*Strangers to
England*

Strangers to England

Immigration to England
1100-1952

Colin Nicolson

"Goe we hens! for ther is an Englisshman sleyn by the Lumbards in Lumbardestrete."
(Thomas Graunt, 1457)

"They [the English] have an antipathy to foreigners, and imagine that they never come into their island but to make themselves masters of it, and to usurp their goods . . ." (Italian, writing in the sixteenth century)

"No Jews; Christianity and the Constitution." (Eighteenth century election slogan)

WAYLAND PUBLISHERS LONDON

IN THIS SERIES:

Frontispiece. An attack on Jews in London, Middle Ages.

Copyright © 1974 by Colin Nicolson
First published 1974 by
Wayland (Publishers) Ltd
101 Gray's Inn Road London WC1
SBN 85340 399 6
Printed in Great Britain by Page Bros (Norwich) Ltd

Contents

Introduction

ON THE EVENING OF MAY DAY, 1517, a shouting mob of resentful London watermen, apprentices and servants swept through the narrow alleyways and streets of Cornhill and Cheapside. Armed with cudgels, stones and boiling water, they broke down the doors of houses and workshops belonging to foreign merchants and craftsmen, destroying looms, bales of cloth and furniture and flinging the debris into the street below. Their particular target was the house of John de Meautys, a rich French merchant, who was particularly hated as a symbol of alien intrusion and competition. A group of notables, led by the statesman Sir Thomas More, and including the Mayor and Sheriffs of the City, was showered with stones and refuse, and the mob, raising the traditional cry "clubs and 'prentices", continued on its path of destruction. Any foreigner who fell into its hands was beaten, or suffered what was perhaps the worse fate of a ducking in the "Channel" – the stinking and disease ridden open sewer which ran through the city streets.

The young king, Henry VIII, was safe at Richmond, but the Chancellor, Cardinal Wolsey, fearing perhaps that the rage of the mob might turn against him, fortified his house and awaited events behind locked doors. Towards evening, the Lieutenant of the Tower believed that the situation had become so serious that he ordered his artillery to bombard the City. In fact, the authorities had exaggerated the seriousness of the riot, and by the small hours of the morning, the rage of the Londoners had spent itself. Having shown their traditional contempt and hatred of the foreigner in a feast of looting and arson, the crowds began to disperse to their homes.

The events of "Evil May Day" 1517 are easily explained, and fill the twentieth century observer with a depressing sense of familiarity and forboding. "The English are great lovers of themselves, and of everything belonging to them," wrote a Venetian visitor a few years before the May riot. "They think that there are no other men but themselves, and no world but England; and whenever they see a handsome foreigner, they say that 'he looks like an Englishman,' . . . and when they partake of any delicacy with a foreigner, they ask him, 'whether such a thing is made in their country.'"

In the early years of Henry VIII's reign (1509–47), London was full of foreigners, many of whom had settled in the city, maintaining themselves in exclusive ghettos and displaying their wealth in an ostentatious

Opposite. An artist's impression of Evil May Day, 1517, when London apprentices and others attacked foreigners and their property.

and arrogant fashion. The alien and the immigrant seem to have played a disproportionate part in the life of the state; foreign courtiers surrounded the young king; foreign merchants and financiers dominated the commerce of the capital; foreign craftsmen and artisans introduced new techniques which brought them great profit and prestige.

While the Crown encouraged these aliens, popular complaints about their presence were frequent. Foreign merchants controlled the import of continental silks, wines and metals and used their wealth to buy up English products and export them at a profit. Foreigners intercepted food on the way to the capital and resold it to their own profit and the detriment of the inhabitants. The skills and techniques of foreign craftsmen threatened the native craftsmen, and the strangers "set naught by the rules of the City."

On the eve of the May riots, two incidents occurred which further inflamed feeling against the alien community; both bore the stamp of the classic formula for national and racial hatred. First, a group of alien financiers involved in raising an Imperial loan from English merchants went bankrupt and fled the country, ruining a large number of English creditors. A short time afterwards, a Lombard called Francesco de Bardi seduced the wife of an English merchant, and humiliated him when he tried to make her return. These incidents were a sure recipe for antagonism and revenge, and when a group of foreigners gathered at Court, boasting and jesting about Bardi's exploit, they received an ominous warning from an English merchant; "By the Mass," he swore, "we will one day have a day at you, come when it will".

"Evil May Day" was the savage culmination of centuries of English hostility to the strangers who came to these shores, whether as visiting travellers and merchants, or as permanent settlers. Throughout the Middle Ages, the chief way in which we can detect the presence of aliens is through the records of impositions placed upon them, or through descriptions of the violent incidents which took place when the English struck out against their presence.

I *The Royal Milch Cow*
1100–1500

IN OCTOBER, 1290, a party of poor English Jews, carrying all their possessions and their Scrolls of the Law, boarded ship at the mouth of the Thames. This was not a pleasant excursion, but a bid for survival. The King, Edward I, had threatened that any Jews who had not left the country by November 1st would be put to death without mercy. Casting anchor at ebb-tide, the vessel set sail with its miserable cargo, but almost immediately ran aground on a sandbank. At the invitation of the Master, the passengers stepped down over the side of the tiny vessel onto the sand to stretch their legs, and perhaps to take a last look at the land which had sheltered their people for over two centuries since the Norman Conquest. To their horror, the Jews turned to see the vessel refloated, and the jeering crew dividing their possessions amongst themselves. As the tide rose around the doomed men, women, and children, the Captain told them to call upon Moses, who might be persuaded to part the waters for them, as he had done for their forebears.

The expulsion of the Jews in 1290 was the tragic culmination of the history of Medieval English Jewry; this was the most coherent and clearly defined community of immigrants to be found in England before the arrival of the Protestant refugees of the sixteenth century. While the comings and goings of Norman, Angevin, Aquitainian and Gascon knights and merchants are submerged in the shifting sands of the Post-Conquest Anglo-Norman community, the Jews stand out as conspicuous aliens, segregated from the native population by law and by religion. In many ways, their story is a tragic caricature of the relationship between the English and the various alien groups which were to arrive on these shores during the next nine centuries.

Jewish Community in England

The Jewish community in England seems to have had its origins in the Norman Conquest and in the massacres which swept the Continent on the eve of the First Crusade in 1096. From the reign of Henry I (1100–35) onwards there is evidence that considerable numbers of Jews had crossed the English Channel, and by the time of Henry II (1154–1189) there were Jewish communities in London, Lincoln, Winchester, Cambridge, Thetford, Northampton, Bungay, Oxford and Gloucester. At the time of the expulsion, in 1290, contemporaries estimated that the Jewish

population of the country was about 16,000, scattered throughout the land in about twenty-seven centres.

The majority of English Jews came from Northern France, and while many of them spoke Norman French, even amongst themselves, and even used French equivalents for their Hebrew names, they remained a very distinct and unassimilated group within the English community. The most obvious mark of exclusiveness was the distinctive badge which Jews were compelled to wear, sewn into their clothing in a prominent place. Edward I spelt out this obligation in a decree of 1275: every Jew, male and female, was to wear a piece of yellow taffeta, six fingers long and three broad. This regulation was enforced with much more rigour in England than elsewhere in Europe. It meant that the Jews stood out everywhere as conspicuous aliens in the general population.

Attacks on the Jews

Outbreaks of savage violence against the Jews were common in medieval England – a result of religious fanaticism and economic stresses. The earliest of these outbreaks, which was by far the worst example of its kind in early medieval Europe, occurred in 1189–90. At the Coronation of King Richard I, certain Jews, despite the religious taboos forbidding it, entered the Cathedral during the Coronation service. This caused a riot in which some thirty Jews were murdered, and the entire London Jewry burned down. Worse was to follow; the King's departure for France for six months to gather his forces for a Crusade was the signal for an onslaught against the Jews throughout the kingdom.

By far the worst tragedy occurred at York, which had sheltered an immigrant Jewish community since at least 1130. The local barons were heavily indebted to the Jews, and it appears that when they heard of the destruction of the London Jewry, they saw a chance of wiping out their own debts by the brutally simple method of murdering their

Jews in medieval England were compelled to wear distinctive badges.

Opposite. Jewish merchants in medieval England. There were 16,000 Jews scattered through England at the time of their expulsion in 1290.

Left. Jews being burned alive in Germany. It was from such terrors that Jews fled to England in the Middle Ages.

Nineteenth century view of what was a Jew's house at Lincoln in the Middle Ages. Such large houses were often built for self-preservation rather than a desire to impress.

creditors. Material gain combined with Crusading fanaticism was a potent brew. The barons, led by one Richard Malbysse, whose reputation had given him the nick-name "The Evil Beast," burst into the house of one of the principal Jews of York, murdering his wife and setting fire to the building. The rest of the terrified community took refuge in the keep subsequently known as Clifford's Tower. By the evening of 16th March 1190, the keep was surrounded by an overwhelming and hostile force, and the fate of the 150 men, women and children who had taken refuge there seemed to be certain death.

A tragic climax to these events now took place. Urged on by their Rabbis, the desperate Jews decided to imitate the heroic example of Masada; rather than face the fanatical onslaught of their former neighbours, they burnt their valuables, set fire to the building, and put themselves to the sword. The fears of the Jews had not been misplaced, for when the few survivors opened the gates and ventured out in the dawn, they were set upon and butchered to a man.

In many ways, it is not surprising that the York massacre occurred in England, for such outrages were common here. The Jewish community of Bury St. Edmunds was wiped out when fifty-seven people were massacred on Palm Sunday, 1190. In 1262, John Fitz-John, one of Simon

de Montfort's most ruthless followers, led an attack on the London Jewry; after murdering the wealthy and respected Jew, Isaac fil'Aaron with his own hands, Fitz-John let his followers loose on the Jewry in an orgy of destruction which cost scores of lives. These were but a few examples of the numerous persecutions which took place between the arrival of the Jews after the Conquest and their expulsion in 1290. For the Jew, England was perhaps the most dangerous and insecure land in which he could find himself. There were two main reasons for this; England was the home of the pernicious "Ritual Murder" accusation which gave rise to bitter anti-Semitic feeling, and the hatred of Englishmen was turned against the Jews because of their occupation as money-lenders.

Savage attacks on Jews were common in medieval England. Firing and sacking a synagogue.

The "Ritual Murder" Legend

On the eve of Easter, 1144, there occurred the first recorded example of the accusation that Jews stole Christian boys and used them for evil religious rites. The body of a young apprentice was found in a wood near Norwich, and somehow a rumour spread through the area that the youth bore the marks of crucifixion. People began to believe that the

A church for converted Jews, London.

13

Jews had crucified him, in a gruesome mockery of the Easter Passion of Christ. The affair caused a violent reaction against the Jews, and it was only with difficulty that the Sheriff of Norwich kept the peace. This affair laid the foundation of a potent legend that was to rear its head constantly through the ages, until it gained a new dimension at the time of the Nazi persecutions. Every few years after the incident in 1144, fresh accusations were made which added to the ignorance, suspicion, and hostility which existed between the Jewish immigrant community and the English. At Gloucester in 1168, the Jews were said to have tortured a child named Harold and thrown him into the River Severn. Similar accusations were made at Bury St. Edmunds in 1181, and at Bristol in 1183.

By far the most serious of these recurring incidents occurred at Lincoln, in 1255. In August of that year, Jews from all over the country had assembled in the town to celebrate a wedding. On the day after, the body of a little Christian boy called Hugh was discovered in a cesspool near one of the Jewish houses. The owner was seized and tortured until he "admitted" that the crime had been committed by the wedding guests. At once a storm broke over the heads of the Jewish community. Nearly a hundred of them were arrested and thrown into prison to await trial, and later several were summarily executed because they refused to accept a wholly Christian jury. The "martyred" Hugh became the centre of a religious cult; his remains were carried in a huge procession to the Cathedral, where he was buried in a splendid shrine. The tomb was still believed to be capable of working miraculous cures at the time of the Reformation.

Jews as Money-Lenders

There is no doubt that legends of this sort, which are given no credence by modern historians, put great strain on the precarious relationship between Gentile and Jew. As such episodes became part of folk memory and popular culture, remembered over a century later by Geoffrey Chaucer in the *Canterbury Tales*, they gave powerful stimulus to racial hatred and religious prejudice. Popular distrust, combined with the vindictive and frequently proclaimed hostility of the Church, and laws which forced the Jews to live an exclusive and separate existence, were bound to result in friction between the two communities. But there was also a very specific and material explanation for the Englishman's hostility to the Jews. They were not only used as the agent of Royal exaction, but were virtually the only source of credit in the medieval world, and as such brought upon themselves the hatred that has always attended the profession of money-lending.

The main occupation of the Jews in England, from the time of the Conquest until their economic ruin just before the Expulsion, was money-lending. Ever since the rise of Christianity, the laws of the Church had forbidden Jews to own land, to employ or have any authority over Christians, or to carry arms. This meant that almost every profession was closed to them, but since the Church had also forbidden Christians to undertake usury, the Jews found that lending out their money at interest was the only field left where they could make a living.

Above. Propaganda illustrating the "Ritual Murder" accusation against Jews. Jews were accused of stealing Christian boys and using their blood for evil religious rites.

Below. Satire on the Jews showing them as evil money-lenders. Jews were virtually the only source of credit in the Middle Ages.

Aaron of Colchester, one of
many Anglo-Jewish financiers
who grew enormously rich on
the profits of usury, i.e.
money-lending.

16

It was during the reign of the first Plantagenet, Henry II, that the Jews first established themselves in England as a highly organized financial group. Operating as consortia, Jewish usurers were able to finance a multiplicity of activities, ranging from the purchase of a cow, to a military campaign. Armour, books, agricultural produce, jewellery – all were thrust upon them as pledges to secure the credit that was so essential to everyday existence. Churches and monasteries raised loans by pledging their plate, their Gospels, Decretals, and works of theology, while it was claimed that many a student ruined his career at Oxford University when he pawned his books to the ubiquitous financiers. The most important transactions involved the pledging of land, houses and rents, and it was these activities, sometimes bringing about the ruin of families and the loss of birthrights, which led to most of the friction and hatred between the immigrant community and the English.

Such were the profits of usury that many of the Anglo-Jewish financiers of the twelfth and thirteenth centuries grew enormously rich. When Aaron of Lincoln died in about 1166, he was probably the richest man in the kingdom in terms of liquid assets; his fortune amounted to £15,000 – equivalent to three-quarters of the annual income of the Crown from all sources. Aaron's sons would see nothing of this huge fortune, however, for under the special laws applied to the Jews, the whole sum passed to the Crown. A ship, loaded with bullion taken from the coffers of the dead financier was dispatched to France, where the old king, Henry II, awaited his unexpected windfall impatiently. It was nevertheless Aaron's ghost who was to have the last laugh in the affair, for in February, 1187, the treasure laden vessel was sunk by a storm in mid-Channel, depositing Aaron's entire fortune on the sea-bed.

Jews and the Crown

It was not often that an inheritance as large as Aaron of Lincoln's passed to the Crown, but it is clear that the monarch benefited greatly from the presence of the Jews in the realm. The Jews of England were designated "servi cameri regis," or Serfs of the Royal Chamber, a status that carried with it many privileges; their religion was safeguarded; they were protected against violence, having a right to refuge in Royal castles in times of disturbance; they were allowed to travel through the country without hindrance, although they could not leave it without special permission; they could call upon Royal officers to assist them in collecting debts, and they could sue their debtors in the Royal courts. Above all they were the only people in the country who were expressly authorized to lend out money at interest.

The other side to this catalogue of privileges was the fact that the King expected to profit from almost every aspect of a Jew's life. Over and above the taxes that were levied at every stage of their business transactions, the Jews had to pay for permission to move house, to be married or divorced, to employ a Christian nurse for their children or to attend a wedding in London. Even if a Jew became a Christian convert, his property still passed to the Crown at the time of his death. Moreover, the social activities of the Royal family were liable to ensure the Jews

Scenes from the Crusades.
Rich Jews were frequently
ordered to contribute to the
expenses of Crusades.

18

further expense; if a member of the Royal Family married, or if the Queen was confined with child, or if the king returned safe from a journey, the Jewish community was required to register its congratulations in terms of hard cash.

Not content with these regular exactions, the Crown began, towards the end of the eleventh century, to impose crippling arbitrary taxes on the Jews which would lead to the eventual ruin and expulsion of the community. The first of these exactions was the so-called Saladin Tithe of 1186, when the Jews were ordered to pay one-quarter of their property to the Exchequer. This levy was assessed at £60,000, a vast sum equivalent to perhaps £10,000,000 in modern values, and gives some idea of both the wealth of English Jews and the ruthless way in which the Crown was prepared to exploit their wealth.

Perhaps the most unfortunate victim of the Crown's rapacity was Aaron of York, the greatest Anglo-Jewish financier of the thirteenth century, as Aaron of Lincoln had been of the twelfth century. At every crisis of his reign, Henry III (1216–1272) turned to Aaron with open palms. In 1243, he had to provide 400 gold, and 4,000 silver marks on the marriage of Richard of Cornwall; in 1248, Aaron was fined 1,000 marks, and two years later a further 4,000, on a charge of forgery. It was said that the King even stooped to taking gold from the unfortunate financier with his own hands. When Aaron died in poverty, it was estimated that the Court had received from him over 30,000 marks in silver and 200 in gold during his lifetime.

It was obvious that this saga of extortion and exaction could have only one ending. As time passed, the demands of successive monarchs became more unreasonable, and the ability of the Jews to meet them grew less. Methods of collecting taxes grew more cruel and merciless. On the one hand, the English Jewries became progressively impoverished, making them less profitable to the Crown, on the other the Jews were forced to apply greater ruthlessness and pressure to their clients in order to raise the cash to meet the constant Royal demands; "never was it more true," writes Cecil Roth, "that the Jews were like a sponge, sucking up the floating capital of the country, to be squeezed from time to time into the Treasury; while the king, high above them and sublimely contemptuous of their transactions, was in fact the arch-usurer of the realm."

Statutem de Judeismo, 1275

When Henry III died, in 1272, the condition of the Jews in England had been transformed. The prosperous community which he inherited at the beginning of his reign had been reduced by his exactions to a state of ruin and demoralization. He left his successor, Edward I (1272–1307), a serious problem, which could only be solved by drastic remedies. The method put forward by Edward to solve the Jewish problem was to issue the Statutem de Judeismo. This decree, published in 1275, forbade Jews on any pretext to lend money for interest, ordered that their places of residence should be restricted, and that every Jew of both sexes should wear the "badge of shame."

The Statutem de Judeismo took away, at a stroke, the main source of

Henry III. He and other kings exploited the wealth of Jews through heavy taxation and other means.

livelihood of the thousands of Jews living in England. As compensation, the Jews were allowed for the first time to become merchants and artisans, and to have restricted ownership of land. In theory there was no reason why Jews could not make a living on the same footing as Englishmen. In practice of course, this was impossible; Edward made the same mistake that was made centuries later when American slaves and Russian serfs were freed from restriction – economic emancipation cannot take place without social emancipation. The Jews could not operate in English society as equals, for in any attempt to take their place as soldiers, merchants, farmers or craftsmen, the Jews were hampered by constant and explicit reminders that they were outsiders. They were forbidden to enter merchant and craft guilds; they were refused the protection and freedom of movement that was essential to commerce; above all, any attempt to transform the Jew's way of life, while at the same time increasing his isolation and insecurity, was doomed to failure.

Expulsion of the Jews, 1290

Far from being transformed into industrious farmers, craftsmen and merchants, the Jews were driven to desperation by the sudden removal of their only source of livelihood. Many were forced by their plight into illegal usury, clipping the coinage, and even highway robbery. It became clear to Edward that only one solution remained to him. The Jews were no longer a source of wealth to the Crown; their function as money-lenders had been taken over by Christians towards whose activities the King turned a blind eye; their presence in the kingdom as infidels was an affront to Edward's zealous Christianity. The time had come, he decided, to expel the Jews from his kingdom altogether. By 1st November, 1290 the last of them had left the country. Nothing remained of the once affluent community which had made its home in England for the previous two centuries but empty houses and deserted synagogues.

Edward I. Ruined financially by previous English kings the Jews were no longer useful to the monarchy as a source of finance. Edward I therefore expelled them from the country in 1290.

The contribution of the Jews to English life had been considerable. They had fulfilled an essential function in providing a system of credit in a society where banking and usury were forbidden by the Church. It was Jewish capital which oiled the machinery of English medieval society, and it was to the Jews that men turned to defray the expenses of litigation, to pay the "scutage" that absolved them from military service, to pay for a wedding, or to finance a pilgrimage. There is no doubt that, but for the availability of Jewish capital, the two chief public activities of the medieval world – building and warfare – would have been severely restricted. It is ironical that so many of the great edifices of medieval England – the soaring Cathedrals and abbeys, the massive granite castles, which symbolized the majesty of the medieval Church and State – should have been financed by the capital of despised infidels and outsiders.

The story of the Jews in medieval England is almost a caricature of the experiences of subsequent waves of alien immigrants. The English almost always greeted strangers with hostility and even violence, but rarely with the hysterical pogroms experienced by the medieval Jews. It has been usual to blame immigrants for the hardships and grievances of everyday life, but the unique religious and economic position of the Jews made their role as scapegoats doubly uncomfortable. The time taken by immigrants to become assimilated has varied greatly, according to the resilience of their own cultures, but the Jews were unique in that their own exclusiveness was compounded by laws which cut them off from the native population by a sort of medieval apartheid. Until the nineteenth century, governments had an unashamed belief that the immigrant was there to be exploited; his skills and expertise were to be used, and preferably stolen, and his everyday existence was to be made to drip gold from the cradle to the grave. In the case of the Jews this process was pushed to its ultimate – they were used, sucked dry, and then thrown out altogether.

Immigrant Craftsmen

The Jews are unique in the history of immigrants and aliens in medieval England. They stand out as a distinct group, clearly marked out by law, and made conspicuous by the discriminatory treatment they received. The duration of their residence in the country is also clear-cut, because they were forbidden to leave without special permission. Nor are we in any doubt about where they lived, because their residence was determined by the government regulations. All these things give us a clear picture of the Anglo-Jewish community which makes the obscurity surrounding the other alien groups in the country all the more tantalizing.

Certainly, there were foreigners living in the country throughout the Middle Ages, and some of them no doubt became permanent settlers. Royal marriages to members of the foreign nobility usually brought an influx of alien courtiers and favourites, like the swarm of avaricious Savoyards and Provencals who accompanied Eleanor of Aquitaine, or the Frenchmen, Bretons, Lombards, and Navarrese who came in the train of Joan of Navarre – consort of Henry IV. The Church was also a frequent source of alien visitors, and in 1325 Edward II decided that there were so many foreign monks congregating around the coasts that they posed a danger to his security, and he ordered them to move inland.

One sort of immigrant who was welcome by the Crown was the skilled foreign craftsman. In an age when industrial progress depended upon manual skill rather than machinery or technology, it was essential for monarchs to attract craftsmen who were masters of new techniques. As early as 1113, Henry I had encouraged Flemish weavers to settle in Pembroke and Cardigan. Two centuries later, Edward III, taking advantage of unrest in Flanders, saw an opportunity to stop the decay of the English cloth industry. "All the cloth workers of strange lands," proclaimed an Act of 1337 "of whatsoever country they be, which will come to England . . . shall come safely and securely, and shall be in the King's protection and safe conduct, to dwell in the same lands choosing where they will." Many foreigners answered Edward's invitation, and by the end of the fourteenth century we find alien weavers in South Wales, London, Winchester, Norwich, Bristol, Abingdon, and York.

The Alien Population in England

While we catch glimpses of the medieval immigrant in Royal decrees and Exchequer records, the picture we have of him is murky and indistinct. How many aliens were there? Where did they live? How quickly were they accepted by the English? The answers to these questions are lost in the mist of intervening centuries. Suddenly, however, in 1440, a chance of history allows us a view of the English alien community which is extraordinarily revealing. In that year the king, Richard II, desperate for fresh revenue to replenish his empty treasury, decided to tax all the aliens in the country. By medieval standards the tax was assessed very efficiently, and it amounts virtually to a census of the alien and immigrant population. For the first time we are given an insight into the numbers, origins, and distribution of the fifteenth century immigrant.

The total alien born population, in a survey which excludes only

Doche immigrants to England in the Middle Ages – i.e. Flemish, Dutch, Germans and Brabanters – were usually skilled craftsmen such as weavers (*above*) and goldsmiths (*opposite*).

wealthy merchants and the servants of great houses, was about 16,000, or about 1 per cent of the population. Contemporaries, with a logic that was far from being peculiarly medieval, were convinced that the total numbers were much greater. This was because the immigrants were concentrated in certain areas. Over 10 per cent of them lived in London, and the rest tended to congregate in the coastal areas of the South and West. There were for instance, alien communities in over 120 centres in Devon, and twice that number in Kent.

These fifteenth century immigrants appear to fall into four main groups: Irish, Scots, French and "Doche" – a comprehensive term applied to those who came from the Low Countries and North Germany. Each of these groups tended to concentrate in a particular area of the country. London and East Anglia were, for instance, mainly given over to Lowlanders and Doche. The majority of French congregated in Kent, while Berkshire seemed to attract the Irish. The Scots were found mainly in Yorkshire and Northumberland.

Many of these immigrants seem to have adopted English surnames which either denoted their place of origin, as with the case of Peryn Frenssham, Patrick Yrish, or Sebet Docheman, or to have chosen out-landish nick-names based on their appearance or their job – Arnold Wanderfayn, Joanna Walleye, or Katerina Inkepottis. It is to be hoped that the name of Isabella Manswoman, a Yorkshire vagabond, denoted not her occupation, but the fact that she came from the Isle of Man.

The occupations listed in the taxation returns give some idea of the contribution these aliens made to the English way of life. The Doche – Flemish, Dutch, Germans, or Brabanters – were engaged almost exclu-sively in skilled crafts such as weaving, leather-making or brewing. There were also many tailors, goldsmiths and glaziers among them, while a letter from an Essex villager to his friend in London gives us an insight into another Doche occupation. The letter asks if the friend would look for a "mason that is a ducheman or a flemyng that canne make a dowbell chemeney of brykkes – for they canne best fare there . . ." He goes on to make an understandable provision for his chimney: "I would have seche as cowde maket wele to voyde smoke." It is perhaps significant that it was to the expertise of a "Doche" craftsman that the man turned in his smoky dilemma.

While the Doche immigrants were skilled craftsmen and artisans, the Irish and Scots worked almost exclusively as herders of sheep and cattle, although there were some Irish parish priests and clerks. Some French-men were also engaged as herders, but most of them, particularly the Normans, worked in skilled trades as builders, smiths, millers, weavers, or brewers. There were also a few aliens from the Mediterranean coun-tries, many of whom were employed as physicians. Men like Thomas Frank, a Greek who later became a naturalized Englishman, and the Spaniard, Fernand de Melonia, came to England as "doctors in medecyns" because of the well-known shortage of university men in the country.

The taxation returns of 1440 give us a brief, but extraordinarily vivid glimpse of the fifteenth century immigrant population. They constitute a record of the numbers, distribution, and activities of the alien com-munity that is unique in medieval Europe. But it must be remembered that these records refer only to those aliens who were not merchants, for merchants were exempted from the tax. But it was those aliens who were not engaged in commerce who were most likely to become per-manent residents in the country and are therefore most relevant to the story of immigration to these shores.

Foreign Merchants

It was not, however, the humble Flemish weaver, plying his trade in some dingy workshop, who attracted the attention and the hostility of the Englishman, but the flamboyant wealth of the foreign courtier or merchant. From the time of the Norman Conquest, England's overseas trade was dominated by foreigners, and alien traders flocked to the rich English market from all corners of Europe – Venetians and Genoese, with silks, velvets and spices, Flemings and Dutchmen with linen cloth, Spaniards with iron, Norwegians with tar, Gascons with wines, and

Opposite top. A doctor applies herbs to a patient's eyes. Many aliens from Mediterranean countries were employed as doctors in England.

Opposite bottom. Irish and Scottish immigrants worked almost exclusively as herders of sheep and cattle.

French immigrants were mostly skilled workers, such as millers (*above*) and blacksmiths (*below*).

The Peasants' Revolt, 1381.
Aliens were made a special
target by the rebels.

A German Hanse merchant of the "Steelyard" ghetto in London. Foreign merchants frequently attracted the hostility of the English because of their great wealth.

Germans with furs and amber. On the whole, English kings encouraged these adventurers with grants of protection and privilege, and by the fifteenth century there were colonies of alien merchants in most of the great ports and cities. The most important of these merchant ghettos was the "Steelyard" in London, where the merchants of the German Hanse had their own churches and warehouses, and even their own guildhall.

Few of these merchants became permanent residents in England. Indeed, there were laws which limited the length of their stay, and forced them to lodge with English "hosts" so that their activities could be more closely controlled. But the presence of these rich interlopers brought out all the traditional xenophobia of the English. All aliens, whether they were rich and arrogant Hanse merchants, or humble craftsmen who wanted nothing more than to be left in peace to settle into their new homes, became victims of occasional outbursts of anti-alien feeling.

Attacks on Foreign Merchants

The corporations of English towns waged a ceaseless battle against the encroachments of foreign merchants, accusing them of unfair competition and illegal practices. Sometimes, as in 1376, when the Commons asked for the banishment of the Lombards, or in 1406, when petitions demanded that all foreigners must leave the country, resentment took a legal form. But more often it burst forth in violent attacks on foreigners or on alien communities. On these occasions the blind fury of the mob made little distinction between the crafty foreign merchant who drove up prices by hoarding grain, and the innocent and useful immigrant.

At Boston in Lincolnshire, a group of Flemish merchants were sitting quietly in their hostel after the great fair of 1270, when a mob of Englishmen, incensed by a quarrel between a merchant from Ypres and one from Winchester, burst into the building and dragged the unfortunate foreigners into the street. The Flemings were beaten and robbed, and swords were thrust through their bales of cloth. In the Peasants' Revolt of 1381, aliens were made a special target by the rebels. Suspects were forced to say the words "bread and cheese," a phrase no Fleming, even one who was not threatened with instant death, could be expected to pronounce. There were many Flemings and Dutchmen who died with the words "brod and case" as their banal and unwilling epitaph.

In about the year 1450, a complaint was addressed to the king in a tone which is very familiar to modern ears. The land was over-run, it claimed "with nedy pepyll estrangers of diverse nations, as Frensshemen, Galyman, Picardis, Flemmyngis, Keteryckis, Spanyars, Scottis, Lumbardis, and divers hother nacions, that your lyge pepyll Englisshemen, cannot imagen nor tell wherto, nor to what occupacion, that they shall use or put their children to lern or occupye."

Seven years later, in 1457, a group of Englishmen determined to settle accounts with the alien merchants of Lombard Street, on the grounds that they were "fals extercioners, common lechers, and avouterers [adulterers]." It is significant that sexual fears and jealousies seem to have played an important role in many of these affrays. The signal was given by one, Thomas Graunt, who came out of his shop in Chepe Street, and tried to exhort passers-by to action against the foreigners with the provocative cry "Goe we hens! for ther is an Englisshman sleyn by the Lumbards in Lumbardestrete." Despite the fact that Graunt had the foresight to provide cudgels and staves, with which he invited his neighbours to break the heads of the foreigners, Graunt seems to have found few takers for his afternoon's entertainment, and on this occasion bloodshed was avoided.

Londoners were usually more enthusiastic when it came to an excuse to show their displeasure at the alien presence, as the events of "Evil May-Day" were shortly to show. The stranger, whether he was a Hanse merchant, a Jewish money-lender, or a poor Flemish weaver, was regarded throughout the middle ages with great suspicion and hostility – an interloper who had come to these shores to feather his nest at the expense of the native Englishman. The attitude of the Crown was hardly more enlightened. It encouraged immigrants, but only to exploit their presence unmercifully. Until the sixteenth century, immigrants had been comparatively few in number, but that century was to see the arrival of large numbers of Continental refugees who would put the Englishman's shaky tolerance much more severely to the test.

2 *The Protestant Refugees 1500-1700*

BEFORE THE SIXTEENTH CENTURY, foreigners had come to England for economic reasons. Some of them were merchants, cashing in on the rich English market, others were bankers and moneylenders, who made a living by exploiting the Englishman's lack of expertise and religious scruples in financial matters. On the whole, these men died unwillingly on English soil. Their wills and letters show that they had little commitment to the country, despite long residence. They lived their lives, and enjoyed their leisure, within the confines of the alien community. Their hearts remained in Lombardy, Genoa, or North Germany, and few of them showed any desire to become Englishmen.

The alien artisans and craftsmen of the Middle Ages present a very different picture. Bringing with them only their tools and their skills, these people came to England in response to the repeated invitations of English monarchs, and they came to stay. Despite the hostility of the natives, the trickle of skilled immigrant craftsmen flowing into the country in the centuries following the Conquest, seems to have been absorbed fairly quickly into the mainstream of English life.

In the middle of the sixteenth century, immigration to England was given a new and dramatic impetus. The growth of Protestantism in Europe, and the often violent attempts to stamp it out as a subversive and dangerous heresy, loosed a flood of religious refugees upon sympathetic neighbouring territories. After 1550, large sections of the industrial populations of the Low Countries, Germany and France found that the only way that they could practise their religion in peace was by going into exile.

The situation became acute when Phillip I came to the Spanish throne in 1556; he saw it his duty to mount a determined and bloody assault upon any Protestants living in his dominions, and in 1567 he sent the Duke of Alva to put down the Dutch Protestants by force. Shortly afterwards the Duchess of Parma wrote that 100,000 people had fled from the Spanish Netherlands, and that half the houses in Ghent, the largest city of the Province, lay empty. Meanwhile, in France, the death of Henry II plunged the country into thirty years of confusion and civil war, in which the Protestants suffered terrible persecutions, such as the massacre of St. Bartholomew's Eve, in 1572. The result of these pressures was to unleash a flood of emigré Protestants, comprising the flower of the skilled population of France and the Low Countries, upon Germany, the United Provinces and England.

Opposite. Lord Burghley. He was one of the far-sighted men who recognized the value of Protestant refugees' skills and therefore encouraged them to settle in England.

PARIS

(Der Admiral.

The Massacre of Saint
Bartholomew's Eve, 1572,
when Protestants in Paris
suffered terrible persecution.
Such attempts in Europe to
quash the growth of
Protestantism forced many
Protestants to flee to England.

Neither the English monarchs nor the English people welcomed this
sudden influx. From the point of view of the sovereign, the refugees were
a political embarrassment, further complicating the already delicate
relations with France and Spain, and their extreme Protestantism made
the refugees a focus of religious fanaticism and discontent. For the people
at large, the immigrants were doubly unwelcome; they were regarded
as a potential burden on the native population because many of them
arrived destitute and they were thought to be a potential threat to the
Englishman's livelihood because the bulk of them were craftsmen whose
skills would take away English jobs.

Despite these misgivings, no attempt was made to stop refugees
entering the country, and they were fortunate to find support amongst
a group of powerful aristocrats. Men like Lord Burghley and Lord
Somerset realized that these industrious newcomers could bring great
benefits to the country, and they believe that Protestant refugees had a
right to expect asylum in England. Amidst the storm of popular hostility,
the emigrés were fortunate to find such influential friends.

Beginning as a movement of a few scattered exiles in Henry VIII's
reign (1509–47), dying away briefly under the persecutions of Mary, the
influx of refugees came to a peak in the early years of Queen Elizabeth
(1558–1603). By 1550, three immigrant churches had been established
at Canterbury, London and Glastonbury, and Queen Elizabeth was

quick to grant new letters patent for communities of "fflemyng strangers, dutchmen aylians" all over Southern and Eastern England. One of the earliest of these was at Sandwich, where 406 immigrants were settled in 1561; others were soon established at Norwich (1566), and Southampton (1567), while the majority of the exiles came, as usual, to London. It seems these refugees fell into two main groups: some were Walloons, who came from Artois, Hainault, Namur, and Luxemburg, and spoke French; others were Flemings and Dutch, who came from Flanders and Brabant, and spoke a Teutonic dialect. There were small communities of French at Rye and Dover, and a tiny group of Germans and Italians who came to London. The flow of immigrants continued until the end of the century, when political events on the Continent caused it to cease.

These Protestant refugees did not choose to leave their homes, nor were the English a people who welcomed strangers: "They have an antipathy of foreigners," an Italian observer remarked, "and imagine that they never come into their island, but to make themselves masters of it, and to usurp their goods..." It was unfortunate for the emigrés that their arrival coincided with a crisis in the development of the English economy. The second half of the sixteenth century was a time of frequent depressions which had the usual consequences of increased unemployment and suffering; at such a time an influx of destitute foreigners was bound to cause suspicion and hostility. The refugees came when guilds and livery companies were trying to control trade and to establish restrictive monopolies; newcomers who clearly stood outside the English system were regarded as an impediment to this process. Above all, the paternalist Elizabethan state was determined to centralize and control every aspect of economic life, and to prevent the diffusion of industry to the countryside. The humble Dutch and Flemish immigrants could hardly have chosen a worse time to arrive empty-handed in a strange land.

Immigrant Skills

If most of the refugees had been forced to leave their homes without any material possessions, they were fortunate that they had other gifts to offer their unwilling hosts. The relationship between Protestantism and industrialization has fascinated generations of historians since a connection between the two was suggested by R. H. Tawney in his seminal study *Religion and the Rise of Capitalism*. There can be few better examples to justify Tawney's thesis than the story of the Protestant refugees of the sixteenth century; almost all of them were skilled craftsmen, and through their energy and drive, a whole range of new techniques was introduced into England for the first time.

Perhaps their greatest gift to the English economy was the technique of weaving the so-called "new draperies"—light, soft clothes which were much more suited to the climate of Southern Europe than the heavy woollen goods that were the traditional products of English manufacturers. The English were delighted at the opportunity to learn the mysteries which had hitherto been the monopoly of their Dutch rivals, and the Queen readily allowed the newcomers to exercise the "faculties

Protestant immigrants introduced a whole range of new techniques into sixteenth century England. Perhaps the most valuable was their technique of weaving light, soft cloths. *Above*. A weaver at work.

of making Bays and Says, Arras, Tapestrey, Mockadoes, Staments, Carsay, and such outlandish commodities as hath not bene used to be made within this, our Realm of England.'' Soon, in towns throughout the country, alien weavers were growing rich on the profits of their skills.

Weaving was only one of the variety of crafts that the refugees brought with them to England. Figures of 1616 show that over 121 different trades were being practised by them; they were credited with the establishment in London of glass engraving, and of new potteries; silk weaving was begun in Canterbury, and thread making at Maidstone; immigrants brought printing, linen weaving, and the making of glazed tiles to Norwich; the elaborate ruffs that were so much a mark of the Elizabethan age were fashioned by them. At Colchester, they began the manufacture of parchment and needles; they made places like Newport Pagnell, Aylesbury, and Stony Stratford, centres of the craft of lace making, while a school for teaching the art was established at Great Marlowe.

Certain skills were deliberately attracted by far-sighted men like Lord Burghley, who saw in the troubles of the refugees an opportunity to develop the resources of the country. Aliens skilled in the manufacture of paper, canvas, salt, and soap received a special welcome. Lord Humphrey made great efforts to establish the manufacture of brass, introducing Germans to mine for copper and calamine stone, and establishing a wire-making works at Tintern in Gloucestershire. It is probable that improvements in the manufacture of knives at this date were due to a settlement of Flemish cutlers at Sheffield, under the auspices of the Earl of Shrewsbury, while the start of the cotton industry has been attributed to the arrival of refugees who fled to Manchester

Protestant refugees practised over one hundred trades in England. For example, lace making (*opposite right*), wire making (*left*) and needle making (*below*).

Aliens skilled in tanning (*right*), paper making (*below*)
and other important industries were especially welcome
in England.

after the sack of Antwerp – previously a centre of cotton manufacture.

Leather work was a very important alien craft, indeed there were more of them engaged in this activity than in any other, working as tanners, cordwainers, cobblers, shoemakers and saddlers. Others were involved in the metallurgical trades, particularly in gold and silver work. During Elizabeth's reign, there were about 150 Flemish and German smiths, about 20 jewellers, and 50 precious stone setters working in London.

Another field in which the exiles were well represented was that of gardening and horticulture, and much of the technical development of English agriculture in the seventeenth century can be attributed to their influence. Refugees brought the cultivation of "roots" to East Anglia, and made Norwich famous for its variety of horticultural produce and for new varieties of flowers, such as carnations, provence roses, and gillyflowers. The Lowlanders also used their expert knowledge in the important work of draining the Eastern marshes; a Dutch engineer embodied his plans in a book entitled *A Discourse of Humphrey Bradley, a Brabanter, concerning the Fens in Norfolk*, and many exiles were employed in these projects. No service the newcomers gave to their adopted home was of more value than the re-vitalization of English agriculture through the introduction of new techniques, methods, and crops.

Their contribution to English education and culture was huge, and can only be touched upon here. By their very nature, the exiles were educated and committed men, willing to uproot themselves and to disrupt their lives for an ideal. Indeed their faith was so strong that Flemish and Dutch Anabaptists were willing to be burned for it, even in England. Many of the refugees found work as tutors at Court or in noble households, and others entered the Universities. Bucer held the Chair of Divinity at Cambridge. Peter Regious was catechetical lecturer at Oxford. Two successive emigrés taught Hebrew at Cambridge in the late sixteenth century. There were many artists among the refugees, men like Guy de Brès, an expert at painting on glass, and the cosmographer and map engraver Jodocus Hondius, of Ghent, who collaborated with the great Mercator in making one of the earlier maps of England. In general terms, the refugees acted as a catalyst to the growth of English Puritanism, Radicalism and Dissent to an extent out of all proportion to their numbers.

Exploitation of Immigrants

Although the country derived great long-term benefit from the presence of the refugees, the Tudors used every opportunity to make an immediate profit from them as well. They were subjected to double the rate of tax that was levied on the native English, and also had to meet other irregular impositions, such as the "loom money" they paid at Canterbury for the privilege of being allowed to ply their trade. Various special duties were placed on their goods according to the locality in which they lived. They were also subject to numerous extraordinary taxes, like the 107 refugees who were ordered to pay forced loans of £23,000 in 1601.

Left and below. Protestant refugees were important in the development of agriculture and gardening in England.

Right. Initiation of an apprentice. Immigrants were often forced into apprenticeship as a way of overcoming foreign competition.

38

Jealousy and Hostility

As well as greedy treatment by the State, the immigrants had to face the jealousy and hostility of English trading rivals, who put immense energy into restricting alien competition, and into trying to learn the tricks and secrets of immigrant crafts. Much of this effort centred round the question of apprentices, for by forcing the newcomers to take on English apprentices, and by preventing them from apprenticing their own people, the English believed they could overcome alien competition; the newcomers would be forced to divulge their secrets; the manufacture of the "new draperies" would not become an alien monopoly; the immigrants would be prevented from branching out into new trades. English craftsmen were assisted by the great Statute of Apprentices of 1563, which increased the compulsory apprenticeship period to seven years. This meant that foreign master-craftsmen were expected to serve a second apprenticeship under an Englishman, who was often more concerned with learning the foreigner's skills than with teaching him new ones. English merchants also tried to revive the medieval regulations compelling all foreigners to live with a native "host," who supervised the stranger's affairs, and even took a proportion of his profits. The refugees of Norwich were very bitter about this, and wrote a petition complaining it was "a thing neither the Jews nor Turks do at any time offer to the Christians nor the Christians to the Turks, or to any other nation be they never so barbarous."

The frequent and heart-rending complaints of English craftsmen point to the fact that many aliens simply ignored all these restrictions, safe in the knowledge that their skills were so valuable to the country that no action would be taken against them. Hardly a year passed without a complaint that the newcomers were infringing the regulations which governed their residence in England. London merchants claimed that aliens were defying Acts passed in the fourteenth and fifteenth centuries by selling goods retail, that they were ignoring the "hosting" regulations, and that they were encroaching upon the rights of traditional English crafts. Whenever a guild or other economic group saw the refugee as a rival or competitor, then conflict developed, opposition arose, and usually some form of regulation was imposed.

In 1571, the authorities of Norwich compiled a lengthy "Boke of Orders" which restricted alien traders with a harshness that was amazing when one considers the transformation the refugees made to the fortunes of that city. In making woollen goods, they were forbidden to use "sweete barrelled butter," but only "ciuyll oyl or whale butter." No alien baker was allowed to bake "anye manner of whight breade at all, but onelye breade of mealle . . . providing allways that suche as syll eate whight breade maye buye it at the Inglishe bakers onelye . . ."

The lives of the immigrants were full of petty restrictions and irritants. They found, in Norwich, that they were asked to pay £14 a year for houses that had been let for £2 before their arrival. They were sometimes subjected to an 8 o'clock curfew. They were only allowed to employ English servants. In times of shortage no alien could buy "anye victuall in the market to endamadge or offende anye inhabitaunt," nor could they "resort to anye inne or tiplinge howses" to drink on Sundays

Immigrants in Norwich were subjected to an 8 p.m. curfew, policed by night watchmen (*above*).

or holy days.

In times of economic hardship the newcomers filled their traditional role of scapegoats for all the sufferings and grievances of the times. In 1591, 153 poor citizens of Colchester accused the strangers of being responsible for a sharp rise in the price of foodstuffs. In London, it was claimed that immigrants were "most dysordered persons who walked late in the streets of the citye, dronken and in greate dysorder." A petition of 1616 sums up the grievances of Londoners in an outburst that has a familiar ring to twentieth century ears. The immigrants, it was complained, had "increased ten for one, so as no tenement is left to an English artificer to inhabite in diverse parts of the cytie and subburbs, but they take them over their heads at a great rate.

"Soe their numbers causeth the enhauncinge of the prices of vittells and house rents, and much furthereth the late disorderly new buildings, which is so burdonous to the subject that his Majestie hath not any worke to performe for the good of his commons (especially in cities and townes) then by the takinge of the benefit of the law upon them, a thinge which is don against his owne subjects by common informers. But their daylie flockinge hithere without such remedie is like to grow scarce tollorable."

Many Englishmen seemed concerned at the effect the immigrants were having upon their environment. The citizens of Norwich complained about the habit refugee dyers had of scouring and washing cloth in the river, with the result that "it doth gather such corruption that it cannot be used as in tymes past," moreover, "the whole ffysshe of ye Ryver" were poisoned. This was nothing, however, compared to the sufferings of the citizens of Southampton: there it was alleged in 1589 that "Baltesor de Mastre and dyvers serge mackers," threw "theare fylthie soppie watter into the stretes," and one John Herant, an alien dyer, was charged with using "more watter than will serve a fowerth part of the town." Such activities were deeply shocking to the sensibilities of the Englishman.

Occasionally, complaints against the "frenssh dogges" as the Londoners inaccurately dubbed the newcomers, gave way to threats and outright violence: "Doth not the world see," asked the writer of a London pamphlet of the late sixteenth century, "that you beastly brutes the Belgians, or rather drunken drones and faint-hearted Flemings, and you fradulent father-Frenchmen, by your cowardly flight from your own natural countries have abandoned the same into the hands of your proud cowardly enemies; and have, by a feigned hypocrisy and counterfeit of religion, placed yourselves here in a most fertile soil, under a most gracious and merciful prince, who hath been contented, to the great prejudice of her natural subjects, to suffer you to live here, in better ease and more freedom than her own people?"

These pleasantries were followed by a warning: "Be it known to all Flemings and Frenchmen that it is best for them to depart out of the realm of England between this and the 9th of July next; if not, then to take that which follows. There shall be many a sore stripe; apprentices will rise to the number of 2,336, and all apprentices and journeymen will down with the Flemings and Strangers."

Refugee dyers were often accused of polluting rivers and town streets with their dirty water.

In fact, there were no serious anti-alien riots in Elizabethan England – certainly nothing to compare with the events of May, 1517 (see p. (see p.   ). There was a threat of trouble in 1570, when a group of local men planned to mount an attack on the Walloons and Flemings at Harlesdon Fair. But the project was revealed to the authorities and ended in a fiasco. More serious was the projected attack on the London immigrant community, which was rumoured to be imminent in the Spring of 1593. Again, the riot was nipped in the bud, despite the following verse which appeared pinned to the door of the Austin Friars Church:

> "You strangers that inhabit this land
> Note this same writing, do it understand;
> Conceive it well, for safety of your lives,
> Your goods, your children, and your dearest wives."

Tolerance

As the sixteenth century drew to a close, and as the flow of refugees from the continent began to cease, a greater tolerance of them seemed to grow up amongst the English themselves. Thus, we find a Dutch hatmaker writing home to his wife in 1573: "You would never believe how friendly the people are together, and the English are the same, and quite loving to our nation. If you came here with half our property, you would never think of going to Flanders." Only one aspect of English life seems to trouble him, for he urges her to "Buy two little wooden dishes to make up half pounds of butter; for all the Netherlanders and Flemings make their own butter . . . here it is all pig's fat." Another young refugee writes to his Grandmother: "We have been at Norwich a little less than two years, where we are living in great quietness and peace, and the word of God is much preached among us."

As early as 1570, the burghers of Colchester wrote to the Privy Council asking to receive a larger settlement of refugees: "We cannot but greatly commend the same strangers to you," they wrote, "for since their first coming hither, we find them to be very honest, godly, civil, and well ordered people; not given to any outrage or excess." In a debate in the House of Commons in 1593, in which Sir Walter Raleigh spoke strongly against the refugees, it was said in reply that, "the riches and renown of the city cometh by entertaining the strangers, and giving liberty to them. Antwerp and Venice could never have been as rich and famous but by entertaining of strangers, and by that means have gained all the intercourse of the world."

Economic Benefits from Immigration

The economic benefits brought by the Protestant refugees seem at last to have been appreciated by the citizens of towns like Sandwich; their presence was "to the great advantage of this town," an observer wrote in the 1590's, "by the increase of inhabitants, the employment of the poor, and the money which circulated; the likewise had the great advantage of their rents being considerably increased." Even the citizens of Norwich seem, despite their short-sighted and ungrateful treatment

Sir Walter Raleigh (*above*) was opposed to refugees coming to England.

of the refugees, to have realized their value to the town and a memorandum was circulated describing "the benefits received in Norwich by having the strangers there."

Assimilation

As the seventeenth century progressed, the Protestant refugees began gradually to give up their jealously guarded independence, and to merge their identity with their English neighbours. Intermarriage between the immigrants and English became more frequent, and the exiles, feeling perhaps that the more militant Protestantism of the seventeenth century was more in tune with their own ideals, began to give up their separate religious identity. In 1704, for instance, the Dutch settlers of Canvey Island, coming to the conclusion that they could no longer maintain their separate way of life, abandoned their Chapel, and adopted en masse the customs and language of their English neighbours. Their action might be regarded as the final step in the assimilation of this talented and useful community. Rarely in the history of immigration to these shores has a group contributed so much to their adopted land, and rarely has a refugee community had to face such undeserved suspicion, hostility and restriction.

The Huguenots (1680–1720)

After the Edict of Nantes which allowed Protestants in France freedom of worship, and the collapse of Spanish attempts to crush the Protestants of the Low Countries, the flow of refugee immigrants to England virtually ceased. Never again would the Protestants of the Low Countries suffer such severe persecution, and between 1629 and 1660, Protestants in France were left in peace.

Finding many careers closed to them, they put their energies into trade and business, many of them becoming very rich in the process. When Louis XIV came to the throne (1643–1715) he seems to have thought that the convictions of the Huguenots had been so dulled by material prosperity that they would now give up their separate beliefs and enter into the mainstream of French life. He decided to try to destroy Protestantism in France altogether.

Despite the advice of his ministers, who realized what a loss the Huguenots would be to France, Louis made it clear that his ambition was to root out Protestantism from his dominions. Alarm spread through the Huguenot community, and some of them, like the wealthy Louis Crommelin, were quick to read the ominous portents, and left the country with all their capital and possessions. It was clear that a new exodus of Protestants was about to begin.

From across the Channel, the kings of England watched these developments with dismay. Both Charles II and James II were striving to secure the friendship of France, and to improve the condition of the English Catholics. The prospect of a new influx of Protestant refugees fleeing from the persecutions of Louis was a serious embarrassment to both these policies. To allow the Huguenots free entry to England would

In 1685 Louis XIV of France (*below*) revoked the Edict of Nantes which had allowed Protestants freedom of worship. Faced with persecution again thousands of Huguenots (French Protestants) fled to England (*above*).

prejudice relations with France, while to keep them out would be unthinkable in the virulently anti-Catholic atmosphere of late seventeenth century England.

As Louis' campaign against the Huguenots became more intense, with Huguenot churches burned, troops billeted on Protestant families and men condemned to the galleys, Charles II found it difficult to avoid making the victims a public offer of asylum. It was the Edict of 1681, lowering the age at which Protestant children could be converted to Catholicism from 12 to 7, that forced Charles to issue a proclamation offering "letters of denization under the great seal without any charge whatsoever, and likewise such further privileges and immunities as are consistent with the laws for the free exercise of their trades and handicrafts," to any Huguenots who cared to come to England.

This proclamation opened the doors to the greatest influx of foreign immigrants the country had yet seen. The English ambassador in Paris wrote of "the joy here upon the news of the care the King is pleased to have of the Protestants who seek refuge in England." Thousands of them made the short sea voyage from the Protestant strongholds on the West Coast of France to London and the ports of the south coast. "They came hither in troops daily," wrote one observer, and added with some exaggeration, "and in the greatest part of them with no other goods but their children." The numbers of refugees swelled to even greater proportions when Louis revoked the Edict of Nantes in 1685, and by the end of the century it was estimated that between eighty and one hundred thousand of them had crossed the Channel.

Welcome Huguenots

The welcome the strangers received was a contrast to the usual English reaction to foreigners. Throughout the country, sympathy for them was reflected in the huge amounts raised on their behalf in Church collections. Five separate appeals were made, and despite the obstruction of James II, the collection for 1686 amounted to nearly £50,000. A generous annual grant was made by Parliament, and this was still being payed until well into the eighteenth century. A group of noblemen and leaders of the Huguenot community, known as the French Committee, was set up to administer all this money.

The majority of the new immigrants settled in the traditional areas of alien predominance – London, and the South and East Coasts. Some of the first Huguenot churches were established in Bristol, Barnstaple, Bideford and Plymouth, and soon there were immigrant communities scattered throughout the south and east of England. Many of them stayed near the coast, where they could carry on the maritime pursuits in which many of them had been engaged at home, others joined existing alien communities in places like Southampton, Norwich and Canterbury. The attitude of government was very different to the centralized paternalism of Tudor England, and there was no attempt to restrict the movement of the refugees. The whole country lay open to their enterprise and energy.

Inevitably, the majority of Huguenots found their way to London. Many of them joined the existing emigré community in Soho, setting up their homes around Cock and Pye Fields in the parish of St. Giles. Soon streets and alleyways echoed to the sound of dozens of craftsmen at work – paper-makers, glass-engravers, makers of fur hats and surgical instruments, bakers and brewers; the cottages and workshops of the newcomers began to spread eastwards to the green slopes which ran down to the Strand from St. Giles Church and the fields above High Holborn.

Spitalfields became another Huguenot enclave, and Londoners complained that it was difficult to hear English spoken there in some streets. In contrast to the grey and seedy slums which later grew up there, Huguenot Spitalfields was a gay and prosperous quarter. Observers were impressed by the splendid gardens which sprang up between the cottages and houses; window-boxes were filled with the dahlias and tulips beloved of the French exiles, and dove-cotes and pigeon lofts were a prominent feature of many of the houses.

It was evident by the turn of the century that most of the exiled Huguenots who remained in England were prosperous and contented, and that they had been accepted by the English with a warmth that contrasted with the reception given to their predecessors a century before. "They made us welcome in their houses," wrote one grateful emigré, "and treated us with affectionate care. Thus has God given us fathers, mothers, brothers and sisters in this strange land." In 1698, there were over 15,000 immigrants receiving charitable relief. By 1696, the Huguenot churches themselves had taken over the care of their own community to the extent that it could be said that "of this multitude of poor exiles, barely 3,000 are at alms."

Arrival of Huguenots in England. Huge amounts of money were raised by many people in England to help the refugees.

The Huguenots built their own churches in England, such as this one in Wandsworth, London (*above*).

Why Huguenots were Welcomed

It is clear from all this that the reception given to these Huguenot refugees was very different to the one received by their sixteenth century predecessors. It is difficult to imagine church collections and government grants for alien immigrants in Elizabethan England. This change of attitude can largely be explained by the changed political climate of the age. The Civil War, and the growth of a more militant Protestantism, had inculcated in the English a fierce hatred of the sort of Catholic absolutism epitomized by the regime of Louis XIV. The English seemed to identify and sympathize with the persecuted French Protestants, whereas their sixteenth century Flemish and Dutch forebears were regarded as a nuisance and a threat. As one contemporary observer put it: "the people of England were more especially liberal on this occasion; because they began to think it might be their own case, and everywhere the effect of Popery and arbitrary power."

There were other reasons for the ease with which this latest influx was assimilated. From the first, it was obvious that many of them were only temporary residents in the country, and it is probable that at least half of the 80–100,000 Huguenots who came to England later moved on to Holland, Ireland or the American Colonies. It seems that, despite the warm welcome given to them, when it came to earning their living many Huguenots came up against the same jealousies and restrictions which had curbed their predecessors; their response was to move to places like America, where their energy and skills could flourish unrestricted. The knowledge that many exiles were only temporary residents must have done much to ease the traditional fears of the native population.

The coming of the Huguenots also coincided with the English Revolution, when James II was replaced by the Protestant regime of William of Orange, an event which was not only favourable to the needs of the emigrés, but was to some extent established by them. Many of the Huguenots who fled to Holland when the persecutions began entered the service of the Dutch government; a college of French cadets was established at Utrecht, and the Dutch army, shattered by the long war with Louis XIV was strengthened enormously by the experienced French Protestant officers who entered its ranks, bringing with them a very high standard of discipline and efficiency. When William of Orange landed in England, in 1688, the backbone of his army consisted of two Huguenot regiments commanded by General Schomberg. Other regiments commanded by the Huguenots La Caillemette, La Mellonière, and Cambon later fought with distinction in the Irish campaign, and were involved in the Battle of the Boyne; large numbers of French exiles later settled in Northern Ireland and did much to strengthen the implacable Protestantism of the province. Huguenots were given prominent positions in William's government, and far from being grudgingly accepted by the regime, the second wave of Protestant refugees were in some ways regarded as its favourite sons.

Despite the favourable political situation, the transitory nature of the immigration, and the sympathy many English people felt for fellow Protestants, the main reason for the remarkably friendly reception was probably economic. The country was more prosperous and more populous than it had been at the end of the sixteenth century, and although the second wave of immigration was much larger than the first, the English economy was also far more capable of absorbing it. What is more, although many of the Huguenots had been forced to leave France empty-handed, nearly all the emigrés were skilled and educated, and a considerable number of them were wealthy men who were able not only to look after and employ their own people, but also to give a considerable boost to the English economy.

The Huguenot Contribution

Like the sixteenth century refugees, the Huguenots were masters of a hundred useful crafts and skills which were grafted onto the English economy to the profit of natives and newcomers alike. Many of them were

Because James II (*above*) wished to promote good relations with Louis XIV of France he looked on Huguenot immigration to England with dismay. But public opinion in England was strongly pro-Huguenot initially.

The Dutch William of Orange, William III of England (1650–1702), strongly favoured Protestant immigrants.

men of great energy and resource, who had been tempered by the struggle for survival in the midst of persecution and insecurity. Such a man was Jacques Fontaine, whose competitive zeal wreaked such havoc among the West Country traders, that they raised shouts of protest reminiscent of the burghers of Norwich a century before. They accused Fontaine indignantly of being "a jack of all trades, being a wool-comber, dyer, spinner and weaver, grocer and retailer of French brandy, hatter, dealer in St. Maixant stockings and dyed chamois leather, and in tin and in copper wares." As was so often the case, the newcomer or inter-loper was able to see a dozen ways of making money which eluded the eyes of the natives, whose enterprise was dulled by years of easy-going trading in the old ways.

The impact of the Huguenots on the technology, business, and finance of early eighteenth century England was profound. The area of technological innovation in which the newcomers made most impact was the manufacture of high-quality and luxury goods. Twentieth century historians who have made detailed studies of the growth of these industries, have emphasized the huge contribution made by immigrants in watchmaking, the production of precision instruments, fine textiles, cutlery, paper and glass.

London Huguenots were involved mainly in the production of high-quality textiles and clothing, much of which had formerly been imported by rich Englishmen from France. In Wandsworth and Southwark they introduced the art of making beaver hats which had been up till then a monopoly of the Caudebec area of France; Londoners described with relish how even the Roman Cardinals were now forced to send to Protestant London for their fur hats. At Richmond and Bromley, craftsmen formerly employed in the great Gobelin factory set up work-shops to produce fine tapestries. Most important of all was the silk industry which sprang up in Soho and Spitalfields, turning out the beautiful brocades, satins, velvets, and silk stockings which the English bought instead of expensive French imports.

Although the English glass industry was already established before the arrival of the refugees, Huguenot craftsmen brought with them the special techniques involved in the manufacture of fine glass for mirrors and crystal. The English paper industry was also already in existence, and the art of making coarser types of paper was well known; what Huguenot emigrés like Dupin, de Vaux, and de Portal brought to the industry was the art of making the fine white paper that was so necessary to printing, the production of letter paper, and most important of all, the printing of paper money.

Another expensive item that the well-dressed seventeenth century Englishman was forced to buy abroad was fine bleached linen, a product that was only made at home in very inferior quality. The arrival of the Huguenots changed all that. In 1697, an Act of Parliament was passed "for encouraging the linen manufacture of Ireland, and bringing flax and hemp into, and the making of sailcloth in, this Kingdom." A year later, Louis Crommelin, who had already shown his acumen by leaving France before the Huguenot persecutions began, was invited to form a Royal Corporation for the linen trade in Northern Ireland.

Glass blowing and spectacle making, two skills which Huguenots practised in England.

Crommelin invested £10,000 of his own money in the project, and
began to attract large numbers of Huguenot craftsmen to his factory
in County Antrim. The Huguenots had much to offer; they knew the
best methods of flax-culture; they could teach fine spinning, and had
the most efficient looms. By 1705, 500 refugee families were established
in Northern Ireland, and a flourishing linen industry there meant
that yet another home-produced product had been substituted for a
foreign import.

Another enterprise in which the Huguenots and other immigrants
played a vital role was in the financial revolution of the early eighteenth
century which transformed English banking. Before the foundation
of the Bank of England in 1696, Dutchmen and other foreigners already
dominated English banking, and by the beginning of the eighteenth
century they had been joined by Sephardic Jews, who had entered
the country in Cromwell's time, and Huguenots who had either smuggled
their capital out of France, or had become rich through their English
enterprises. Forming a compact and enormously wealthy society which
revolved around the Dutch Church at Austin Friars, the Huguenot
Temple in Threadneedle Street, and the Sephardic Synagogue at
Bevis Marks, these aliens were vitally important to the financial life
of eighteenth century England. The centre of their business was
Jonathan's Coffee House in Change Alley, from which a web of their
agents and attorneys spread out to conduct lucrative transactions in
the credit-starved capital, maintaining an important link with that
other great financial centre, Amsterdam, by means of the fortnightly
packet-boat. Many of these immigrant financiers, some of them Dutch-

men or Huguenots like the great East India merchant, Sir Matthew Decker and the bankers Gerard and Joshua van Neck, others Sephardic Jews like the Capadoses, de Pintos, Da Costas and Salvadores, were among the richest and most powerful men in London. In 1745, over a third of all City men had Huguenot, Dutch, or Sephardic names, and there is no doubt that emigré financiers gave enormous assistance to the process by which London was becoming the financial capital of the world.

Like the first wave of Protestant refugees, many of the Huguenots were intellectuals and scientists who made an important contribution to English culture. The great Huguenot academies – institutions like the Ecole de Theologie at Nimes, the Academy at Die, and the University at Saumer – were at the peak of their influence and fame when Louis suppressed them. Hundreds of Protestant academics were forced to flee to England, where many of them formed a brilliant circle around the Duc de St. Evremond. A considerable number of exiles became Fellows of the Royal Society, and some of them showed the tendency to produce brilliant if often impractical inventions which foreshadowed the Industrial Revolution; Denis Pepin produced a pressure cooker which formed the basis for his later plans for a steam engine; Drebbel designed a submarine, which was too far ahead of its time to impress the scientific world of the eighteenth century; Louis Paul patented a spinning-machine which anticipated the principles of Arkwright's "jenny;" John Dolland made important improvements in the design of the telescope and the microscope; the mathematician, Le Moivre was a protégé of Newton, and was said by some to understand the theory of gravity better than his master.

For a comparatively small community, the Huguenots produced an extraordinary number of outstanding men. They were part of a process that was already underway in England – the destruction of an old, conservative and restrictive society, based upon tradition, custom and status, and profoundly suspicious of change. The impact of the Huguenots, who by their industry, enterprise and ingenuity forced themselves into the centre of English economic life, was like a fresh wind blowing away the remaining cobwebs of medievalism, and clearing the way for the Industrial Revolution.

In many ways the Huguenots were ideally suited to the new competitive society that was beginning to emerge in the mid-eighteenth century. Their hard work, ambition and enterprise made them prototypes of the thrusting entrepreneurs who throve in the new ruthless climate.

The Protestant refugees had proved that immigrants could be absorbed easily into the mainstream of English life, and that their presence could be extremely beneficial to the native population. It remained to be seen if less gifted and more dissimilar peoples could expect a different reception.

Samuel Courtauld (*opposite*), founder of the present multinational Courtauld textile company, died in 1881, leaving £700,000.

Part of Hogarth's engraving "Noon" (1738), showing members of the French community in Soho, London leaving church while the English, on the other side of the gutter, indulge in basic pleasures!

56

3 "No Jews, no Wooden Shoes" 1700-1815

IT WAS NOT UNTIL the end of the eighteenth century that the French Revolution sent a fresh wave of refugees fleeing across the Channel. Until 1789, new arrivals fall into three very contrasting categories: Irish, responding to famine and harsh English policies by escaping to the doubtful haven of England itself; Jews, who began to enter the country again in small numbers after 1656; and black slaves and runaways, who, by the end of the eighteenth century, constituted a significant minority.

The Irish

After his brief honeymoon with the Huguenots, the Englishman renewed his contest with the alien as if refreshed by the short rest. Eighteenth century London could be a very uncomfortable place for the stranger. Violence was almost a part of everyday life. Social and political discontent was liable to break out in the form of bloody religious riots, which often turned against the Catholic Irish. The relationship between the employer and his men was often established in trials of strength involving broken heads and copious blood-letting: "Sir," certain journeymen shoemakers amiably addressed their employer, "Dam your blood if You do not Ryes Your Works Too 2 pence a Pair moor We Well Blow Your Braines out . . . if You Doo not Do itt You slim Dog We shall sett You Houes on fier . . ." Hatred and contempt for foreigners also seem to have risen to new levels in mid-century: in 1755, it only needed a performance by some French dancers at Drury Lane to provoke a riot, in which fashionable theatre-goers and groundlings alike were involved in an affray which cost the Theatre owner, David Garrick, £4,000 in damaged scenery, props, and furnishings.

As strangers and Catholics, the small Irish community was doubly vulnerable, and its presence in the country is mainly advertized by occasional outbreaks of anti-Catholic violence, in which the Irish were unwittingly caught up. They were, for the most part, unskilled labourers, engaged in portering, building work, hawking, river work and coal heaving. There were Irish scattered throughout the country, but most of the 14,000 or so Irishmen lived in the London parishes of St. Giles, Holborn, Whitechapel, St. George's and Marylebone. In 1736, and

Opposite. Queen Anne. In 1708 she passed the General Act of Naturalisation by which Protestant refugees were welcome to come to England. The resulting influx of poor, unskilled Protestants, seen above in a camp at Whitechapel, London, led to the speedy repeal of the Act.

D

The small Irish community in London suffered severely during the Gordon Riots against Catholicism in 1780.

again at the time of the Gordon Riots in 1780, the Irish suffered severely, despite the fact that their numbers remained small until the huge migrations of the nineteenth century.

Jews

Another immigrant group that was again becoming significant in the eighteenth century was the Jews. From the time of their expulsion in 1290, there had been no official Jewish community in the country. Certainly, small numbers of Jews lived here during these centuries, but they could do so only by becoming Christians, or by concealing their Jewish faith. At last, in the mid-sixteenth century, first the Protector Cromwell, and later his successor, Charles II, let it be known that Jews could now enter the country again. Soon they had established their synagogue and burial ground, and small numbers of Jews began to settle in the country.

By the 1660's there was a small but flourishing Jewish community in London; Samuel Pepys visited their synagogue, and had his calm

Many of the Jews who fled to
England from persecution in
Eastern Europe and Russia
between 1870 and 1914
continued to live in great
poverty. *Above* A soup kitchen
for poor Jews in Spitalfields,
London. *Below*. Baron Lionel
Rothschild, a member of the
wealthy Jewish banking family
who originally settled in
England at the end of the
eighteenth century.

Huguenot refugees landing at Dover, England in 1685 after the Edict of Nantes had been revoked in France. Artist's impression.

Black servants were popular in eighteenth century and early nineteenth century England. *Above*, a portrait by Pierre Mignard of the Duchess of Portsmouth with a black servant. *Right*, a black servant, extravagantly dressed in the style of the time (early nineteenth century), wards off an unwelcome visitor.

NOT AT HOME, OR A DISAPPOINTED DINNER HUNTER!

Scene in an eighteenth century synagogue in England.

Anglican sensibilities profoundly shocked by the boisterousness of the proceedings: "But Lord!" he complained, "to see the disorder, laughing, sporting and no attention but confusion in all their service, more like brutes than a people who know the true God." Pepys did not realize that he had been watching the festival of the Rejoicing of the Law, which is traditionally a noisy occasion.

At first, only a handful of rich merchant families took advantage of the possibility of settling in England, but by 1720 there were several thousand Jews clustered around the new synagogue which had been opened in 1701 at Bevis Marks. Almost all these early Jewish settlers were Sephardim – exiles from Spain and Portugal who were escaping from the Inquisition. They spoke Spanish or Portuguese, had Iberian names like Da Costa, Periera, and Montefiore, and took pride in the wealth, refinement, and sophistication of their society. An English visitor, John Greenhalgh, was much impressed by the congregation of the Sephardic synagogue, who were "all gentlemen [merchants], I saw not one mechanic person of them; most of them rich in apparel, divers with jewels glittering (for they are the richest jewellers of any) . . . they have the quick piercing eye and look as of strong intellectuals; several are comely, gallant, proper gentlemen. I knew many of them when I

saw them daily upon the Exchange and the Priest too, who is also a merchant."

Early in the eighteenth century, a different type of Jewish immigrant began to enter the country – the Ashkenazi. These were Jews from Eastern Europe who spoke Yiddish – a mixture of German and Hebrew. The new comers were much poorer and more puritan in their religious beliefs than their predecessors. The Ashkenazi soon outnumbered the Sephardi, and set up a separate community around their own synagogue in Dukes Place. By 1800, there were about 4,000 Sephardi, and 20,000 Ashkenazim in the country, forming a community which exercized an influence in banking, finance and business out of all proportion to its numbers.

In 1745, Samson Gideon raised a loan of £1,700,000 which helped to prop up the finances of the monarchy. Jewish immigrant families like the Rothschilds and the Montefiores were among the wealthiest in the country, and Jews dominated the trade in bullion, diamonds and other precious stones. There was another side to the coin, however. Many of the Jews arriving in the country, particularly the Ashkenazi, were unskilled, uneducated and destitute. With no provision for welfare, and in the pitiless climate of the early industrial revolution, these people

Oliver Cromwell was the first English ruler since the expulsion in 1290 to allow Jews to come to England and practise their faith. But discrimination seems to have occurred against Jews under Cromwell, as this petition to him from a number of Jews indicates.

An execution at Tyburn. Eighteenth century London was a rough place for an immigrant to come to.

The Ashkenazim – Jews from Eastern Europe, speaking Yiddish – began to enter England in the eighteenth century. Many were unskilled and uneducated and were forced to earn a living by such trades as peddling (*left*) and buying and selling old clothes (*below*).

were forced to compete with Irish, poor Blacks and the native unemployed in a merciless struggle for survival. By the end of the century, Jewish crime had become a considerable problem, and the richer members of the community were continually embarrassed by cases of pickpocketing, highway robbery, and the receiving of stolen goods. Great efforts were made by them to eradicate the poverty that led to this situation.

Anti-Jewish Feeling

In 1753, there occurred a series of events which showed that, despite appearances, the re-admission of the Jews had not been welcomed by many Englishmen. In that year, Parliament passed a Bill granting full rights of naturalization to the children of Jewish immigrants. Despite the mildness of this Bill, an unexpectedly violent storm of anti-Jewish feeling suddenly arose up throughout the country. Pamphlets urged that lines like "O Pray for the peace of Jerusalem" should be struck out of the Psalms. Bishops were accused of pandering to those who had murdered the Saviour. It was suggested that St. Paul's would soon be turned into a synagogue and that Englishmen would be forbidden to eat pork. The anti-Jewish agitation coincided with an election, and constituencies soon resounded with slogans like "No Jews; Christianity and the Constitution;" even the innocent, clog-wearing Huguenots, who must have thought that they were accepted by this time, found themselves pilloried by the popular cry, "No Jews, No Wooden Shoes." The Jewish Naturalization Act was submerged in this tide of chauvinism and anti-alienism, and the point was made once again that the eighteenth century Englishman, like his Tudor and Medieval ancestor, had an engrained distrust of Jews, "frenssh dogges," "wooden shoes" and any other outlandish being who had the misfortune not to be born on this Island.

The Black Community

Another group that was expanding rapidly at this time was the black population. In order to understand how Africans came to be walking the streets of eighteenth century London, it is necessary to go back several centuries.

Little was known about Africa until the fifteenth century, but the later Middle Ages had abounded in myths and traditions about the continent and its inhabitants. After the Portuguese began to explore the coast of Africa in the fifteenth century, Englishmen like Richard Eden and Richard Hakluyt published accounts of the travels of Portuguese sailors which owed much to imagination and mythology. The Elizabethans were staggered by these accounts; they learned of vast lakes and rivers, of huge beasts like those "which some call an Oliphant," which were of "such huge biggeness" that they were beyond the comprehension of the Englishman. Above all, they learned of the African himself, a being whose blackness, nakedness and alien moral code was so radically opposed to the values of sixteenth century England, that the

mere existence of the African was deeply disturbing to all accepted notions.

In 1555, John Lock brought a small group of black slaves to England. Suddenly the African was no longer a curiosity from the pages of travellers' tales but a living reality in the streets of London. After Lock's voyage, the traffic in black slaves expanded rapidly, and by the end of the century black "servants" were a common sight throughout the country. There even existed a small community of prosperous free Africans, some of whom, in 1597 had the temerity to build their own house in London in defiance of Elizabethan regulations. The number of Africans in the country came to the notice of the Queen herself, and she was not enthusiastic about their presence: "there are of late divers blackamores brought into this realm," she complained, "of which kind of people, there are already here to manie . . ." She believed that "those kind of people may well be spared realme, being so populous," and suggested the solution was that "those kind of people should be sente forthe of the land."

Attitudes towards Blacks

It seems that the Queen's wishes were ignored, for during the seventeenth century, coinciding with the huge growth of the Atlantic slave trade, the black population of England continued to expand. By the end of this period the attitude of the English towards the black man seems to have undergone a fundamental change. Before the slaving expeditions of men like Sir John Hawkins, the very concept of slavery had been foreign and indeed abhorrent to the English. As the British captain Richard Jobson told an African slave trader, the English "were a people who did not deal in any such commodities, neither did we buy or sell one another, or any that had our own shapes."

One of the many black sailors on English ships during the eighteenth and nineteenth centuries.

Black servants were widely employed by the rich in eighteenth century England, but there was always a fear of their supposedly excessive sexual appetites.

In 1783 Lord Mansfield (*above*) judged a case where a negro slave had been thrown from an English slave ship (*below*), and concluded that it "was the same as if horses had been thrown overboard."

A cynic might say that this attitude to slavery came easily to the English because their economic system had no need of slave labour at this time; but soon the insatiable demands of the New World made slaving the most profitable of all commercial enterprises, and the English attitude to the black man underwent a surprising change. Gradually, the African came to be regarded as a commodity of trade — as goods or merchandise. The Royal Charter of 1663 gave to the Royal African Company "the whole, entire and only trade for the buying and selling of any negroes, slaves, goods, wares, merchandises whatsoever;" as late as 1790, an Act of Parliament could refer to "Negroes, household furniture, utensils of husbandry or cloathing;" in 1783, Lord Mansfield concluded, in a case where Africans had been thrown from the slave ship *Zong* in mid-Atlantic, that it "was the same as if horses had been thrown overboard."

The African community of eighteenth century England thus lay beneath a double burden. The attitude of the general public had been

so distorted by the mythology and prejudice of past centuries, that Africans were regarded as possessions and subhumans; even the law of the land seemed to confirm this view. It is not surprising therefore, that the story of the African in Stuart and Hanoverian England is not a happy one.

Serving the White Man

It is not easy to assess the size of the eighteenth century black population; contemporaries differed widely in their estimates of total numbers, and their guesses were often distorted by emotion and propaganda, but the black population was certainly not more than 20,000. Their main area of concentration was London, where there were large black communities in Mile End, Paddington, and along the River; Bristol, Liverpool, and Cardiff also had their black areas, and black "servants" were found in great houses throughout the country.

Most blacks had, in fact, arrived as slaves. Ships' captains returning from Africa and the West Indies were allowed to import a few slaves to sell as a personal bonus; others were brought in by retiring plantation-owners, businessmen or officials. Some arrived in the country as stow-aways, fleeing from the back-breaking labour of the plantations; others deserted their ships to take advantage of the comparatively humane climate prevailing in England. After the American War of Independence, there was an influx of black slaves whose Loyalist masters were escaping from the new American Republic. By one means or another, the black population of England continued to swell throughout the eighteenth century.

A large proportion of blacks in England, therefore, were slaves, although their masters preferred to call them "servants." It was not only their black skins that marked them out, but the magnificent uniforms which most of them wore; the English gentleman intended the extravagant liveries of his black servants to reflect his own exalted position in society. Black servants were arrayed in all the finery that the eighteenth century wardrobe could provide – red waist-coats, silver buttons, powdered wigs, and the finest silk shirts. Were it not for the metal slave-collar that all black servants wore around their necks, one might have taken them for their masters. It was as if, by clothing their slaves in this splendid apparel, the English gentlemen could mask the embarrassing realities of their real status as household slaves.

Many of the negroes who were most conspicuous in eighteenth century society were engaged in the business of entertaining the white community. Two of the greatest bare-knuckle fighters of the age, Bill Richmond and Tom Molineux, were black, and became the idols of the sporting world, patronized by the Prince of Wales and Lord Byron. (It is worth noting that several of the other notable pugilists of the last part of the century – Daniel Mendoza, Samuel Elias, Isaac Britton and Abraham Belasco – were Jews.)   Other English blacks who could broadly be described as entertainers were Macomo, the great lion-tamer, and Harriet, who became renowned as one of the most successful prostitutes of eighteenth century London. Inevitably it

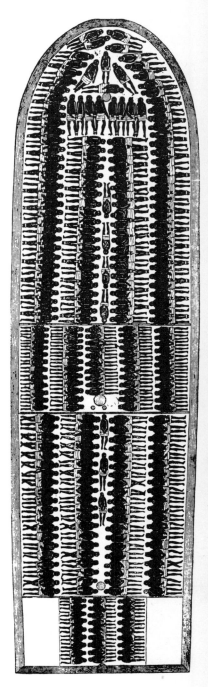

Most negroes arrived in England as slaves, packed together in the ships like any other cargo, as illustrated below.

Molineux.

seemed, in the eighteenth century as in the twentieth, the successful negro found himself pushed into his age-old role of pandering to the amusements of white society.

There were some black Englishmen who broke out of the social bonds constraining them, and they were outstanding men by any standards: Job ben Solomon, a highly educated Fulani tribesman, who was abducted into slavery and only freed when he came to the notice of the Governor of Georgia, became for a while the darling of intellectual society in London; Ignatius Sancho, who was brought up as an Englishman and wrote plays, music and poetry which were highly thought of in Johnsonian London; Olaudah Equiano, nicknamed Gustavus Vasa, was another freed slave who devoted himself with great energy to improving the lot of his less gifted comrades – a work in which he collaborated with another outstanding African, Ottobah Cuguano.

These men were the exception, however, and most black people in England were either slaves or menial labourers. Increasingly, more and more of them began to break away from this degraded and hopeless existence and escape to the refuge of the great cities. It is possible that contact with poor whites like themselves had shown them that their bondage was not an act of God, nor a mark of their inferiority as a "species." Certainly, they were more likely to try to escape than their brethren in the New World. These "runaways" led a miserable and insecure existence, constantly expecting to be recaptured and returned to a life of slavery. It was impossible for most of them to earn their living because of the need to avoid recapture, and the fact that rigorous craft and guild regulations prevented them from practising their skills or from learning new ones. Their only future was to huddle in poverty amongst their own people, in the hope that communal solidarity and the anonymity of the city would save them from recapture.

Poverty and Hopelessness

In such circumstances, poverty and hopelessness was the lot of most negroes in England; at the end of the century their condition had become such a social problem that the government was forced to set up a special fund for relief of the black poor. Not surprisingly, many of them turned to begging and vagabondage as their only hope of survival, and groups of black tramps became a common sight on country roads, driven from parish to parish in an endless search for food and shelter. Others turned to crime, and cases of negroes who were imprisoned, transported, and executed were a common occurrence in the courts.

In the violent climate of eighteenth century England, it is perhaps surprising that there is no record of friction or violence between the black community and the poor white population. Perhaps it was because the condition of the black population was so bad that they could not be regarded as a threat to white living standards. Perhaps it was because the unskilled negro could not compete, as the Protestant refugees had competed, with the white artisan or craftsman class – that section of the community that was jealously aware of its economic status and always liable to react violently to any threat to it. Whatever the explanation, there were no serious explosions of racial violence even in the degrading slums of eighteenth century London.

Fear of Black Men

If an unexpected harmony reigned between black and white poor, there was no shortage of educated citizens who prophesied disaster for the country (as James Walvin has shown in his book *Black and White*).

Some black Englishmen broke from the social bonds constricting them. Ignatius Sancho (*opposite*) wrote plays, music and poetry, highly thought of in eighteenth century London.

DRAME

COMEDIE

VERITE

POESIE
ODE

ROMAN

FABLE

IGNACE SANCHO

M.elle Coiquet Sculp.t

CLERGET

The conditions of the black
community got steadily worse
through the eighteenth and
early nineteenth centuries.
Many had to resort to beggary,
like Joseph Johnson (*right*), a
black sailor who wore a model
of the ship *Nelson* on his head.

It was the influx of negroes after the American War of Independence which intensified many fears and unleashed a wave of panic and alarmism; the city of London had, according to one observer become "lately infested with American negroes;" another fearful commentator, exaggerating the facts out of all proportion, claimed that 40,000 slaves had entered the country after 1772; a foreign traveller was convinced that the country was being overrun by "a little race of mulattoes [half-casts] as mischievous as monkeys." It seems that many Englishmen, noticing the Blacks more because of their colour, were making the common mistake of hugely over-estimating their numbers. The volume of pamphlets published show that they were convinced that the traditional English way of life was about to disappear in an uncontrolled black tide. In fact, the negroes formed a tiny proportion of the total population, and by 1850 there was scarcely a black face to be seen in the country.

Another reason for the fears of some Englishmen was the growth of mixed marriages between the races. The overwhelming majority of the black population was male, and this tended to increase white fears. The absence of black women made it inevitable that marriages and sexual relationships between black and white were common. There was no shortage of people who foresaw disastrous consequences in this, and ignorance about genetic laws, which show that mixed races tend to display the strong qualities of both, led some people to fear the growth of a debased and inferior race, "till" in the words of one alarmed critic, "the whole nation resembles the Portuguese . . . in complection of skin and baseness of mind."

A general disapproval of sexual contact between the races did not prevent the public from treating with great relish any such scandal involving a member of the aristocracy. The Duchess of Queensbury's infatuation with her black servant Soubise, upon whom she lavished her wealth and educated as a gentleman, received enormous attention in the Press. Caricaturists and cartoonists always welcomed such affairs as an opportunity to employ their talent for leering inuendo, displaying the white man's age old obsessions and fears about the sexual prowess of the African.

The Mansfield Judgement, 1772

As the eighteenth century progressed the condition of the black community grew steadily more desperate, but, in 1765, an event occurred that was to have profound consequences for their future. In that year a black youth called Jonathan Strong, his head streaming with blood, staggered into the surgery of a Doctor William Sharp in Mincing Lane. The boy was suffering from serious injuries, caused when his master had beaten him savagely about the head with a pistol-butt for some trifling misdemeanor. By chance, the doctor's brother, Granville Sharp, happened to come into the surgery while the boy was receiving treatment. Sharp was so outraged by what he saw, and by the fact that the law gave virtually no protection to blacks in circumstances like this, that he became from that day a relentless crusader for the improvement of the condition of the black population.

A band of black street singers, early nineteenth century.

The fundamental need, as Sharp realized, was to make clear the legal status of the black population. The laws relating to slavery in England were ambiguous, and judges, fearful of the social upheaval that would follow emancipation and of the wrath of slave-owning Establishment, were reluctant to clarify it. At last, in 1772, after a long period of polemics and judicial delay, a judgement was given by Lord Mansfield in the case of the runaway slave, James Somerset; the Mansfield Judgement seemed to confirm Sharp's contention that slavery in England was illegal: "The exercise of the power of a master over his slave," said the Judge, "must be supported by the laws of particular countries; but no foreigner can in England claim a right over a man; such a claim is not known to the laws of England . . . the claim of slavery can never be supported. The power claimed never was in use here, or acknowledged by the law."

The Mansfield Judgement did not end slavery in England. There is evidence that some rich Englishmen continued to own slaves well into the nineteenth century, and planters continued to kidnap runaway slaves and forcibly transport them to the colonies. But no Englishman who owned slaves could any longer feel secure, either morally or legally, that his right to do so would go unchallenged.

Decline of Black Population

If the legal position of the blacks in England was improved by the Mansfield Judgement, their material position continued to deteriorate. The army of black unemployed was swelled by large numbers of runaways who now had the backing of the law, and there was an influx of American ex-slaves after the American War of Independence. The black "servant" could no longer play the role that he had been imported to fill – English law had taken away the footstool upon which the blacks had served the English, just as it had taken away the counting-table of the Jews centuries before.

By the end of the century the black population had begun to decline, until by 1850, virtually no blacks were to be found in the country. Some of them were sent as free labourers to the West Indies; a few black settlers went to Sierra Leone, where a colony of freed slaves was set up; but the bulk of the black community, which consisted almost entirely of men, gradually merged with the general population through inter-marriage. There was to be no further addition to their numbers until the twentieth century.

The French Revolutionary Exiles

At the time when the condition of the black population was becoming acute, the country was suddenly subjected to a large-scale influx of a very different nature. In May, 1789, the summoning of the Estates General by Louis XVI began the long epic of the French Revolution. Over the next few years England became a haven for nearly 80,000 refugees from France, and although virtually all of them returned with the restored Bourbons in 1815, the sheer size of this Royalist influx makes it worthy of brief comment.

In one week nearly 1,700 emigrés landed at Brighton, and another

1,300 at Eastbourne, many of them after great hardship and danger. The Duc de Liancourt was hunted for weeks through Northern France before he managed to set sail for England under the noses of a search party. The Comptesse de Saisseval crossed the Channel in an open boat in the depths of winter, and narrowly escaped drowning. The English government, despite its hostility to Revolutionary France, was far from enthusiastic about receiving into the country masses of fanatical Royalists, especially as revolutionary agents could easily be smuggled in under the guise of emigrés. They were forced to make some provision for the two Bourbon Princes, the Compte de Provence (later Louis XVIII) who was established at Hatfield House· and the Compte d'Artois (later Charles X) whose stay at Hollyrood House was mainly distinguished by the use he made of its high walls to hide from his creditors.

Other, less distinguished exiles, like the poet and novelist Chateaubriand, who nearly starved in London, had little assistance from the government. Some of them were welcomed into the houses of English aristocrats, but most had to rely entirely on their own resources for survival. The ways in which some of them were forced to earn their living contrasted strikingly with their leisured existence during the Ancien Regime. A few of them used skills acquired to while away the boredom of afternoons at Versailles, and became dancing-masters or fencing instructors. Others were forced to take up more menial positions; instead of reading novels in the cool library of his Chateau, M. Gautier de Brècy catalogued books; the Chevalier de Anselme employed his knowledge of the good life by working as a waiter in a London restaurant; instead of holding elegant discourses with his peers in the Hall of Mirrors, the Marquis de Montazet was reduced to cleaning windows; the unfortunate Marquis de Chavannes became a coal-man.

In 1793 the government passed an Aliens Act which restricted the entry of French emigrés, and caused several of them, including Talleyrand, to leave the country in haste. On the whole, those remaining did not approve of their temporary refuge. Enduring the tedium of exile in London suburbs or in the depths of rural Norfolk, or forced into the humiliating experience of earning a living in unaccustomed ways, they complained endlessly about the climate, the food and the barbarity of their English hosts. As soon as Louis XVIII was ponderously resettled on his throne, almost all of them lost no time in shaking the English dust from their feet. Some of them would be forced to suffer exile again in 1830 when the incompetent Charles X, once more exchanged the Court of France for Hollyrood and his Scottish creditors.

By 1816 nothing remained of the French exile community, but its presence had convinced many an Englishman that he was uniquely tolerant of foreign political refugees, and that England was indeed, in the historian Macauley's phrase, "the Sacred Refuge of Mankind." This was to become one of the most cherished beliefs of Victorian England — an article of faith that few would dare to challenge. It was not destined to be put to the test until the beginning of the twentieth century.

4 *Myths and Realities 1815–1905*

The "Open Door"

FROM THE TIME OF THE FRENCH REVOLUTION onwards, England became a refuge for political exiles, ranging from Ultra-Royalist French aristocrats to revolutionary Marxists. The Industrial Revolution had plunged England into an era of unparalleled expansion and prosperity, and in this climate the country could well afford to accept a scattering of emigrés who posed no threat to the living standards of the mass of the population. The ruling classes found it refreshing and flattering to patronize foreign liberals, who were struggling against autocracies which made mid-nineteenth century England seem in comparison a veritable Utopia. A comfortable feeling of fair-play was maintained by the acceptance of a succession of burnt-out monarchs and autocrat ministers, who were allowed to eke out their days harmlessly on British soil.

We have already mentioned the tide of emigrés from Revolutionary and Napoleonic France which washed briefly over the country after 1789, and then receded as quickly in 1815. The fall of Napoleon, and the restoration of autocratic regimes all over Europe, led to the influx of a new type of refugee – European liberals fleeing from the reaction on the Continent. Many Englishmen were overwhelmed with feelings of sympathy for Greek and Italian Revolutionaries whose politics would have met with their strong disapproval if they had been expressed by an English radical. The poetry of Byron, who "dream'd that Greece might still be free" the aura of antiquity and the emphasis placed in English education upon the classics, go far to explain the romantic mist through which the English viewed the politics of Greek independence. The immense weight of the classical and medieval past gave an equally rosy glow to the successive fiascos of the Italian independence movement. Exiles from Greece and Italy, and also from Spain and South America were common in the 1820's and 1830's, and refugees like Mazzini and the brilliant Antonio Panizzi, father of the modern British Museum, were welcomed with open arms into the homes of liberals like Jane Welsh Carlyle, who made her Chelsea home a haven for exiles. When an abortive Act was passed in 1825, seeking to limit the flow of continental emigrés, it was claimed that nearly 25,000 of them were resident in the country at this time.

Poets and writers helped form nineteenth century opinion in favour of foreign revolutionaries. The poet Lord Byron (*above*) "dream'd that Greece might still be free."

Opposite. Irish emigrants to England.

83

From the French Revolution through the nineteenth century England was a haven for political exiles, such as Louis Kossuth (*above*), Giuseppi Mazzini (*right*), Louis Philippe (*below* with friends) and Victor Hugo (*below right*)

The Revolutions of 1848 led to yet another wave of Continental emigrés. First to arrive were the defeated standard-bearers of the old régime, Metternich, Guizot, and Louis-Philippe, who landed under the pseudonym "Mr. Smith" to begin a second exile across the Channel. Shortly afterwards, the revolutionaries themselves began to join their former rulers in exile, as, all over Europe, the forces of reaction began to re-assert themselves. Karl Marx, who had participated in the revolution by word rather than deed, began a long residence in North London, marked by an unending struggle to overcome poverty, and a continuous outpouring of philosophical and revolutionary ideas, stemming from hours of relentless study in the Reading Room of the British Museum – a creation of a revolutionary exile of another era, Antonio Panizzi. Many other casualties of the failed revolutions were allowed into the country, which believed itself to be prosperous and confident enough to fear nothing from them: Frenchmen like Ledru-Rollin, Louis Blanc and Victor Hugo, Poles like Count Worcell, Hungarians like Louis Kossuth, who replaced Garibaldi as the darling of English Romantic Liberalism – all were brought safely under the umbrella of tolerant hospitality.

In 1870, the fall of Napoleon III in France meant that there was yet another change in the composition of the exile community. While Republicans like Victor Hugo, who had languished for twenty years in the Channel Islands, sailed eastwards to a triumphant welcome in Paris, the defeated remnants of the Second Empire, including Queen Eugenie, the Prince Imperial, and later the Emperor himself, were heading towards England. The government installed the Imperial family at Camden House, near Chislehurst. Although Napoleon himself had only a few months left to live, the Empress remained in England until, at the age of over ninety, she was buried beside her husband and son in Farnborough.

Not only the Imperial family, but also members of the defeated Paris Commune were welcomed in the years after 1871. They were followed by exiled German socialists like Edward Bernstein, Russian anarchists like Prince Kropotkin, and most distinguished of all, Lenin, the father of the Russian Revolution. A continuous stream of political exiles came into the country throughout the nineteenth century. They were few in number and not many of them remained in the country all their lives, but it seemed as if a fine tradition of political tolerance had been established, and that any politician who tried to interfere with it would be certain to incur the displeasure of the British public. As one M.P. proclaimed, the Englishman "clings to the right of asylum; he will not permit it to be touched with impunity any more than the right of public meeting and the freedom of the press."

These assumptions were put severely to the test, however, by the sudden arrival of successive waves of poor immigrants, whose numbers and poverty made them seem a real threat to the living standards of the English working class. First to arrive, beginning in the 1830's and swelling to a huge tide with the famines of the 1840's, were the Irish. Hardly had their numbers began to slacken, when in 1882 a flood of persecuted East European Jews began to pour off the immigrant boats. How did

Starvation and poverty forced two-thirds of Ireland's population to emigrate in the nineteenth century. An Irish hovel (*opposite top*), starving peasants at the gates of the workhouse (*opposite bottom*), and Irish emigrants leaving for England (*above*).

the nineteenth century philosophy of tolerance and the "open door" stand up to these pressures?

The Irish

There had always been a small but steady stream of immigrants across the Irish Sea ever since medieval times. Cities like Bristol, which had an Irish settlement before 1200, and Liverpool, which had an Irish population of nearly 2000 in the seventeenth century, had always attracted Irishmen, sometimes as seasonal workers and sometimes as permanent settlers. As we have seen, the Irish in the eighteenth century formed a minority of sufficient size to incur the displeasure of the London mobs, but it was in the nineteenth century that immigration from Ireland began to assume huge proportions. Soon the Irish immigrant population in itself would be many times larger than all other immigrant groups added together.

As was usually the case, the forces that pushed the Irish out of their native land were stronger than those that attracted them to England. Only rarely in her history has England been a country which offered sufficient opportunities to attract settlers in the way the United States or Australia has done. The typical immigrant to England has been a refugee, either from religious or political persecution, or from intolerable economic conditions at home. In many ways the Irish were as much refugees as the Huguenots.

Why the Irish Came to England

To explain why over half the population of Ireland was forced to emigrate in the century after 1820 is to enter into a tragic catalogue of suffering and injustice. The figures alone are so staggering as to be scarcely believable. As early as 1728, some three or four thousand people were already leaving the country, mainly for Canada and the American Colonies; by 1790, these numbers had risen to nearly 20,000 a year; in the century after this the population of Ireland was nearly halved, and by the 1890's two-thirds of the people born in Ireland were living outside the country. Ireland has exported more of her population in relation to her size than any other European country.

Living Conditions of Irish Immigrants

By far the greatest proportion of the five million Irish who emigrated between 1820 and 1910 went to the United States, but England, only a short boat-trip across the Irish Sea, also received large numbers of them. Some of them prospered in the expansion which accompanied the Industrial Revolution, but most Irish immigrants came to a life that was hardly better than the one they left behind. The towns to which they made their way – London, Glasgow, Manchester, and Liverpool – were experiencing an uncontrolled and unplanned growth under the pressures of rapid industrialization and an influx of poor people from the countryside. As John Jackson observes, "the Irishman who fled from

The "Rookery" in London where many impoverished Irish lived. Farm animals kept in their houses and in the streets were the cause of much disease.

starvation, eviction, and poverty found all too often that he had ex-changed his rags and tatters for a bed of sores in the . . . stench of a cramped and overcrowded cellar in Manchester, St. Giles, or Glasgow."

The system of town administration that had existed before the Industrial Revolution was quite unable to deal with this explosive growth, and new cities spread like vast smoke-blackened camps around the little eighteenth century towns. Thousands of immigrants from the countryside huddled together in hastily thrown-up terraces of cheap houses, without medical care, sanitation, or schools. Into these appalling slums poured an ever-increasing stream of half-starved Irish peasants who had spent their whole lives in the countryside. In many ways the lot of these people was even more miserable than it had been at home,

An Irish wake or funeral party.
The corpse was often kept in
the house long after death.

for in these unfamiliar industrial slums they were cut off from all those
things that had made life bearable, even in the midst of starvation – their
countryside, their Church and their neighbours.

Not surprisingly the Irish, like all previous waves of immigrants,
clustered together in clearly defined areas of the great cities. Typical of
these Irish ghettos was "the Rookery," an area lying around what is now
Tottenham Court Road and Charlotte Street in London. These mean
and narrow streets had been an Irish area since the eighteenth century,
and they were notorious for their overcrowding, filth and crime. A large
proportion of the population lived in damp airless cellars without light
or ventilation. Pigs, donkeys, and starving dogs jostled with unemployed
labourers, ragged children, and old men whose only solace was drink or
gambling.

Curious visitors who dared to take a stroll through these miserable
streets were shocked that such poverty could exist only a stone's throw
from the fashionable world of Mayfair and Piccadilly: "Rows of crum-
bling houses flanked by courts and alleys, culs de sacs etc. in the very
densest part of which the wretchedness of London takes shelter," wrote
one amazed visitor to "the Rookery." "Squalid children, haggard men
with long uncombed hair, in rags with the short pipe in their mouths,
many speaking Irish, women without shoes or stockings – a babe at
the breast with a single garment, confined to the waist by a bit of string;
wolfish looking dogs; decayed vegetables strewing the pavement, low
public houses, linen hanging across the street to dry . . . In one house a
hundred persons have been known to sleep on a night."

Things were scarcely better in the Irish quarters of the other great cities. In Liverpool, a doctor described how he "found . . . a court of houses, the floors of which were below the public street, and the area of the whole court was a floating mass of animal and vegetable matter, so dreadfully offensive, that I was obliged to make a precipitate retreat. Yet the whole of the houses were inhabited!"

Mortality rates among the Irish immigrants were very high, partly due to the frightful conditions in which they lived, and partly because of certain practices which led to a high rate of fatal disease. Animals were kept in their houses, contributing to the general filth and lack of hygiene. Animal dung was kept in huge piles near to water supplies and cooking facilities, so that diseases were transmitted and food poisoned. There was also the unfortunate Irish custom of keeping corpses of people who had often died of contagious diseases for long after they should have been buried, either because relatives could not afford a funeral, or because of the Irish habit of holding "wakes" or funeral parties.

This practice could lead to revolting and dangerous conditions in overcrowded immigrant tenements. A doctor wrote of the shock he received when he went into an Irish house to visit a patient: "a horrible stench arose from a corpse which had died of phthisis twelve days before, and the coffin stood across the foot of the bed . . . This was a small room not above ten feet by twelve feet, and a fire always in it, . . . being the only one for sleeping, living and eating in." The custom of keeping corpses led to a familiarity with death that was spiritually healthy, but physically dangerous and even fatal: "The body," a clergyman relates, "stretched out on two chairs, is pulled about by the children, made to serve as a resting place for any article that is in the way, and is not seldom a hiding-place for the beer bottle or the gin if any visitor arrives inopportunely."

Irish Employment

In his employment as well as his housing, the Irish immigrant tended to occupy the lowest rung of the social ladder. Many of them were not true immigrants at all, but seasonal workers who returned to Ireland when they had earned enough to survive through the winter. William Cobbett described how he saw "hundreds of squalid creatures tramping into London . . . without shoes, stockings or shirts, with nothing on the head worthy of the name of a hat, with rags hardly sufficient to hide the nakedness of their bodies." In 1841, even before the famine swelled their ranks, there were said to be 57,000 of these seasonal labourers in the country, and there was considerable resentment amongst English workers over the way in which the Irish were used as cheap labour to push down wages and break strikes. The pay of these seasonal labourers – perhaps £10 for a summer's work, was hardly enough to keep them alive, and many like the Negroes and Jews before them, turned to begging. Of 15,000 vagrants recorded in 1815, a third were Irish.

The strongest and most fortunate of the Irish immigrants became "navvies," earning good wages by building the vast network of canals and railways that covered the face of nineteenth century Britain. This was a task equivalent to constructing a thousand Pyramids, and many of the men who slaved to dig the cuttings, throw up the embankments, and bore the tunnels which were the sinews of the Industrial Revolution were Irishmen. Many were men of amazing strength, and the ability to work from dawn till dusk without slackening. The strongest of the navvies thought nothing of moving twenty tons of earth in a day, often working underground, soaking wet, and with only a flickering tallow candle to light their way. The navvies were paid comparatively well, but few could stand the back-breaking toil for more than a few years, and accidents and disease meant that the life of a navvy was often short.

Apart from seasonal work and railway construction. Irish immigrants could be found in all types of unskilled and semi-skilled work. Some became dockers, virtually taking over the ports of London and Liverpool by the end of the century. Others went into the cotton factories, working for a pittance at tiring, boring work from six in the morning till eight at night. The British Army was another source of employment, and by the end of the century 15 per cent of British regiments were made up of Irishmen. Thousands more went into the building trade, and helped to construct the factories, warehouses, and workers' cottages that were essential to the growth of industry. Many Irish women supplemented the meagre wages of their husbands by working as domestic servants, laundry workers and street traders.

Attitudes to the Irish

The number of Irish people entering the country by the mid-nineteenth century was astonishing. In 1846, 280,000 of them came into Liverpool, and the next year the figure rose to 300,000. However much they convinced themselves that they would one day return to Ireland, most of these people were in fact permanent settlers, and by 1861, one-quarter of the population of Liverpool was Irish born. How did the English people respond to this Irish invasion?

As we have seen, anti-Irish riots, caused largely by religion, were a regular occurrence in the eighteenth century. In the nineteenth century, the opposition to them became focused upon economic grievances, such as in 1830, when agricultural workers rioted all over Southern England, making the competition of the Irish labourers one of their main complaints. "Randies," or riots between Irish navvies and their Scottish and English workmates, were a common occurrence. At times these became pitched battles with hundreds of railway workers fighting for days and bringing terror to the whole district.

Near one railway site, posters were pasted up giving notice that "all the Irish men on the line of railway . . . must be off the grownd and owt of the countey on Monday the 11th of this month or els we must by the strenth of our armes and a good pick shaft put them off. Your humbel servants, Schots men."

Despite these occurrences, it is the lack of serious communal riots in the nineteenth century, particular in the large cities, which is the most striking aspect of the Irish influx. When one considers the huge numbers of Irish entering the country, and the terrible conditions exist-

Right. An Irish "navvy". Many Irishmen worked as navvies, building England's railway and canal systems.

Below. For most Irish immigrants work was seasonal. When there was no work there was not much to do but hang around the streets waiting for the pubs to open.

ing in the industrial cities, it is surprising that major bloodshed did not take place. Part of the explanation lies in the fact that the economy was expanding at such a rapid rate that the need for unskilled labour was insatiable. It is certain that had it not been for cheap Irish labour, the explosive expansion of industry in the early nineteenth century could not have taken place. On the other hand, the existence of cheap labour may have delayed the introduction of new machinery and methods, and contributed to the decline of British industrial dominance at the end of the century. From the point of view of the English worker, however, expansion and relatively full employment meant that the Irish immigrant posed no serious threat to his livelihood.

Not only were there few anti-Irish riots, but the presence of the Irish did not provoke much articulate criticism. The new industrial workers, unlike the craftsmen and artisans who had opposed previous waves of immigrants, were not sufficiently organized to mount an effective defence of their security of employment. There was insufficient information about social questions such as public health and housing for blaming the immigrant for social distress, and these questions did not become real issues of politics until the end of the century.

Above all, the Irishman was a citizen of the United Kingdom, and as such could not be regarded as a foreigner trespassing on English soil. He was not conspicuous in his appearance, language or dress, and in his poverty he was indistinguishable from the mass of the English, Scots and Welsh working class. The real crisis of Victorian conscience came later in the century, in very different conditions, when a new influx of immigrants, alien in language, religion and culture began to enter the country.

The Jews

Between 1870 and 1914, 120,000 destitute Jewish aliens, fleeing from persecution in Eastern Europe, poured into the country. The English response to their arrival showed that the gracious reception given to a few aristocratic emigrés and intellectuals in the middle years of the nineteenth century had not altered the basic xenophobia of the English.

In 1881 there was an outbreak of savage Jewish pogroms, or massacres, throughout Russia. This was merely the culmination of a series of persecutions which had been taking place all over Eastern Europe for several years. But the events of 1881 convinced many Jews, even those who lived in areas of safety like Austrian Galicia, that the time had come to shake off the insecurity of Eastern Europe and begin new lives elsewhere. Certainly, the period after 1880 constitutes the greatest migration of modern times, and it has been estimated that nearly three million Jews left Eastern Europe in the following forty years.

A long series of massacres, persecutions and injustices swelled the flood of refugees, until at the turn of the twentieth century events brought about a huge exodus. The massacre of Kishinev in 1903, the outbreak of the war between Russia and Japan in 1904, and the Russian Revolution of 1905 sent successive waves of refugees fleeing westwards. For most of them, the United States was the promised land, but huge numbers

Opposite. In most large English cities, Jewish areas were established, such as this one in London.

95

From 1870–1914, 120,000 destitute Jews (*above*) fled from savage persecution (*opposite top*) and massacres (*opposite bottom*) in Eastern Europe and Russia. Many came to England.

F

passed through England on their way to the Atlantic ports, and many
remained to swell the ranks of the small Jewish community which already
existed in the country.

Jewish Areas in the Cities

Like all previous immigrant waves, these refugees concentrated in a
few important centres, clinging together defensively in well defined
immigrant quarters. In the case of the Jews this concentration was even
more marked by their religious exclusiveness and chronic insecurity.

In most large cities, but most notably in London, Manchester and
Leeds, clearly defined immigrant quarters grew up. All these areas were
basically similar in character. They were not areas which were originally working class slums, but rather decayed terraces in neighbour-
hoods which had at one time been prosperous. The Jews showed an
iron determination to remain concentrated almost entirely in these
areas; Whitechapel and St. George's in London; Red Bank and Strange-
ways in Manchester; Leylands in Leeds.

Whole streets were taken over by the newcomers, and extraordinarily
compact and self-contained communities grew up, remaining established
in these poor areas long after the immigrants had become prosperous
enough to move out. When the Jews did move, it was often a case of the
wholesale transplantation of a section of the community, first, in the
case of London to Hackney, Manor Park and Stamford Hill, then to
the more prosperous dormitory of Golders Green in the 1920's, and
finally to the Olympian heights of Highgate, Hampstead and St. John's
Wood. A similar phenomenon occurred in Manchester with the Jewish
ascent of Cheetham Hill.

Much suffering was to take place before these developments, however,
and in the 1880's all Jewish quarters shared one characteristic – they
were situated in the most densely populated and over-crowded urban
areas of the country, at a time when local government was only beginning to cope with the huge problems posed by modern cities. The East
End of London, which became the home of the overwhelming mass of
new arrivals, was in the 1880's by far the most densely populated and
decayed urban area in the world. With a population larger than most
capitals of Europe, East London was a huge rotting sprawl which had
grown up haphazardly during the previous century.

From the City, it stretched endlessly eastwards and northwards, a
formless grey sea of packed terraces, factories and workshops, seething
with poverty stricken humanity. "It was," said Walter Besant, "a city
without a centre, without a municipality, without any civic or local
pride, patriotism or enthusiasm." It was an area where every commodity
and service essential to civilized life was lacking; sewage and drainage
was so inadequate that the smell of decay and disease constantly pervaded
the streets; streets and alleys were so badly lit that pickpockets, thugs
and murderers could lurk undetected in the dim courtyards. It was shortly
after the beginning of the Jewish influx that the notorious Ripper murders
threw into relief the poverty, disorganization, and isolation which made
the East End as different from the well lit streets of Westminster and
Mayfair as were Shanghai or Calcutta.

It was into this huge slum metropolis that the vast majority of the Jewish refugees found their way. The Sephardi and Askenazi synagogues at Bevis Marks and Duke's Place formed the essential nucleus for rapidly expanding Jewish communities. Whole streets were taken over by the newcomers, who were soon able to spend their entire lives within the Jewish community, attending their synagogues, buying their food, reading their own newspapers, even living next to the same neighbours whom they had known in Odessa, Warsaw or Bucharest.

English visitors were amazed at the transformation which had taken place in familiar streets. Bearded and strangely-dressed East Europeans fresh from the ships, women with heads wrapped in huge scarves, a plethora of unfamiliar hoardings, placards and posters – all combined to shock the visitor with a sense of the vivid and unfamiliar. "There are some streets," declared a Conservative M.P., "you may go through and hardly know you are in England." Another M.P. noted with alarm "railway timetables posted in Hebrew characters, the bills of places of amusement distributed in the streets in Hebrew, and the public entertainments given in Yiddish . . . in which were advocated with great impunity all kinds of revolutionary doctrines." English observers were shocked by the speed with which the Jewish quarter grew up, by its air of self-containment and exclusiveness, and by the squalor which both comprised and surrounded it.

As we have seen, the East End of London at the end of the nineteenth century was already one of the worst slums in the Western world before the arrival of thousands of immigrants from the poorest parts of Eastern Europe. Most of these people had little experience of even the most basic requirements of sanitation and hygiene, and their impact on areas whose services were already at breaking point was catastrophic. Piles of rotting refuse accumulated in the streets. Houses which were already overcrowded were filled to bursting-point with new arrivals. Inadequate drainage and plumbing collapsed altogether, and whole streets of houses became malodorous from overflowing sewerage, leaking ceilings, blocked sinks, and walls flowing with damp. These conditions were made more intolerable by the fact that the water supply to the East End was completely inadequate, and was liable to be cut off without warning for hours and even days at a time.

To the amazement of public health officials and government inspectors, these frightful living conditions did not lead to unusually high rates of infant mortality and disease in the immigrant community itself. Indeed, figures in Manchester show that the children of immigrants were better clothed and better fed than those of their English neighbours. Perhaps the Jewish dietary laws, the rituals of religious bathing, and the resilience built up over centuries of hardship, gave the Jewish poor some protection. Certainly, many inspectors were impressed by the efforts of the immigrants to make the best of their unwholesome surroundings, and reports were optimistic about the prospect of future improvement: "The people when they first came over," observed one government paper, "have a different standard of cleanliness from what prevails in this country, but . . . they are amenable to the ordinary methods of sanitary administration."

Jewish Employment

The working conditions of the immigrant were, if anything, worse than those in which he lived. Unlike the U.S., England had little to offer to unskilled and destitute newcomers. The English economy was already highly developed, and there were none of the empty spaces and untapped resources which provided boundless opportunity in the New World. Unemployment among British workers was high, and great resentment was felt against imported foreign blacklegs. The structures of English industry were well established, and its rigid traditions of apprenticeship and industrial hierarchy did not favour the outsider. The welcome from the infant trades union movement was icy. "Yes, you are our brothers," proclaimed the trade union leader Ben Tillett, "and we will do our duty by you. But we wish you had not come."

Above all, this wave of immigrants, coming from the most undeveloped parts of Eastern Europe and Russia, had little to offer their hosts in return for their grudging hospitality. Unlike the Protestant refugees of the sixteenth and seventeenth centuries, they brought no new skills or capital to regenerate the economy. The need for unskilled labour had already been met by the poor Irish who had filled the empty spaces at the bottom of the labour market a generation before. All the newcomers had to offer was a relentless willingness to work for virtually nothing, in order to lift themselves out of the dust. This determination to improve themselves through self-denying toil was bound to cause friction at a time when trades unions were striving to lift workers out of the slavery of *laissez-faire* capitalism by exploiting the bargaining power of labour.

The first, overwhelming problem for the new immigrant was the need to earn his daily bread. Many of them found that the only way they could make a living in the early years was by becoming street pedlars. At a time when retail shops as we known them were only beginning to appear, the wandering pedlar filled an essential need. Ever since the eighteenth century, many pedlars had been Jews; it was from a Jewish pedlar in Piccadilly that Lord Castlereagh, British Foreign Secretary, bought the knife he used to kill himself. The Jewish pedlar became a familiar sight in the country roads and market towns of rural England. Although peddling was a dying trade in late nineteenth century England, many immigrants were forced to take it up as a means of survival. One of them, the Polish Jew, Joseph Harris, wrote his memoirs, which were published when he had established himself as a wealthy Manchester jeweller: "When I commenced business," wrote Harris, "I did not know a word of English. I was taught to say, 'Will you buy?' I did not know what the words meant; I could not understand a word that was spoken to me.... On an average my weekly expenses for some time were about five shillings [25 p.]... My lodgings were from threepence [1 p.] to sixpence [2½ p.] per night, and I managed to get a clean change of bed-linen wherever I stayed ... As for food, I used to buy 1½ lb. of bread, 1 oz. of tea, 2 oz. of butter, and ½ lb. of sugar. The bread and butter served me for supper and breakfast, and what was left I carried in my pocket for dinner. The tea lasted for two days and the sugar for three ..."

Many Jews in London earned their living selling clothes in Petticoat Lane (*above*).

It is significant that the Jewish peddlars found themselves being supplanted by Irish competitors, who, according to Henry Mayhew, were even more desperate than the Jews themselves. "The Irish boy," Mayhew observed, "could live harder than the Jew – often in his own country he subsisted on a stolen turnip a day; he could lodge harder – lodge for 1d. [½ p.] a night in any noisome den, or sleep in the open air, which is seldom done by the Jew boy; he could dispense with the use of shoes and stockings – a dispensation at which his rival in trade revolted; he drank only water, or if he took tea or coffee, it was as a meal and not merely as a beverage; to crown the whole, the city-bred Jew boy required some evening recreation, the penny or twopenny concert, or a game of draughts or dominoes; but this the Irish boy, country bred, never thought of, for his sole luxury was a deep sleep."

Some immigrants trudged the streets carrying glass and ladders trying to scrape a miserable living as window menders. Others set up market stalls in the face of jealous hostility from English market traders, or established themselves as small shopkeepers in the Jewish quarter. For most of them, the struggle to make a living in the early years was relentless and heart breaking.

By far the greatest number of refugees found themselves involved, often within a few days of their arrival in the country, in the so called "immigrant trades." Although the background of the Jews, unlike the Irish, was overwhelmingly urban, few of them were fitted by tradition to go into factories. They preferred to earn their living in small workshops, often owned by a relative or close friend, and employing only a handful of workers in cramped and uncomfortable conditions.

The typical immigrant worker was neither a craftsman nor a modern factory worker. He was engaged in trades – boot-making, cigarette manufacture, above all, the tailoring of ready-made clothes – which were passing through the transitional stage between craftsmanship and factory production. A typical Jewish workshop employed no more than a dozen workers, each of whom was engaged in a small part of the production process. One man might, for instance, be engaged in sewing on buttons, another in stitching collars, yet another in ironing the finished product. It was a sort of mass production without the machine.

This type of production – "sweating," as it became known – was characterized by long hours, dreadful working conditions, and extremely low pay. The nature of the employment, and the inefficiency of the government inspectorate, meant that all sorts of abuses flourished in immigrant employment. To the dismay of social workers and trades-unionists alike, the immigrants themselves seemed not only to endure these conditions willingly, but to resent any attempt to change them.

Working Conditions of Jewish Immigrants

Several reports by the medical journal *The Lancet* in the 1880's gave a shocking insight into the conditions of immigrant workers "In Hanbury Street", observed *The Lancet's* reporter, "we found eighteen workers crowded in a small room measuring eight yards by four yards and half, and not quite eight feet high. The first two floors of this house were let out to lodgers who were also Jews. Their rooms were clean but damp as water was coming through the rotting walls . . . The sink was not trapped, the kitchen range was falling to pieces, while the closet was a permanent source of trouble. A flushing apparatus had been provided, but this discouraged the water outside the pan; the water consequently came out under the seat and flowed across the yard to the wall opposite, which was eaten away at its base . . ."

The Lancet also had serious comments to make about the effect of these working conditions upon the workers' health. The small top room, the report went on, held no less than eighteen immigrants "working in the heat of the gas and the stove, warming the pressing irons, surrounded by mounds of dust and chips from the cut cloth, breathing an atmosphere full of woollen particles containing more or less injurious dyes, it is not surprising that so large a proportion of working tailors break down from diseases of the respiratory organs."

Conditions were hardly better in Leeds, and the report was particularly scathing about one of the workshops it found there. "Entering one of the houses where there are three different workshops, employing altogether about 160 persons, we were assailed by a most appalling stench. There were three closets, the seats and floors of which were besmeared with soil. The sanitary inspector had been here and left word that the place was to be kept clean; but one of the sweaters protested that this was impossible and certainly the warning has had no effect."

Jewish refugees had to scrape a living in England. Many made clothes in dingy slum rooms, working all hours in appalling conditions.

Attitudes to the Jews

It is clear that this influx of destitute and unskilled immigrants would be a severe test of English tolerance. Welcoming these people was a very different proposition from indulging scattered and glamorous liberals in fashionable drawing rooms, putting foreign aristocrats and deposed monarchs out to grass on the banks of the Thames, or indulging the apocalyptic Marxist visions which poured out of Finsbury Park and the British Museum. The Jewish immigrants were poor, unskilled and uneducated. Unlike the Irish, they spoke no English, and came from a completely alien culture. What is more, they came in large numbers, and settled in the poorest areas of cities which already were cracking under huge social pressures. Would English tolerance and the Victorian "open door" survive this onslaught?

For several years after the Jewish refugees began to arrive, it was only the native Jewish community which seemed to be aware of their presence. It was not until 1886 that the Press and a few M.P.'s began to draw attention to the huge changes that were taking place in some of the East End boroughs. By February 1888, Parliament had become sufficiently aware of the problem to appoint a Select Committee of Enquiry, and there were stirrings of anti-alien feelings in the early 1890's. But it was not until after the Boer War (1901), nearly twenty years after large scale Jewish immigration had begun, that the Jewish immigrants became an important issue in British politics.

This sudden awareness of the alien influx was due to two developments; interest had shifted away from Irish and Imperial issues, and fresh waves of immigrants arrived after new persecutions in Russia

Jews carried on their own distinctive way of life in England. A Jewish school in Whitechapel, London.

and Rumania. It was soon clear that the mood of the country was very different to the easy tolerance of the mid-nineteenth century. A group of Conservatives, led by Sir Howard Vincent and William Evans Gordon, M.P. for Stepney, formed the British Brothers' League to press for the introduction of immigration controls, and a hostile and often hysterical campaign was mounted against the Jews.

There is little doubt that there was great discontent in the East End and in many other places where the Jews had settled. They had the misfortune to go to areas where discontent over living conditions and unemployment was already at boiling point. Strangers, whose presence seemed to explain and worsen these conditions, were bound to be treated as scapegoats, and politicians found no shortage of real grievances to fuel their inflammatory speeches.

Like most campaigns against immigration, the speeches and writings of the anti-alien lobby were marked by an outbreak of grandiose and often confused metaphors. Jewish immigrants were likened to "floods," "rivers," "seas" and "swarms of locusts." One writer described them as "the scum washed to our shores in the dirty water flowing from foreign drainpipes;" another saw them as a "smouldering fire . . . eating away at the very vitals of the Metropolis;" epithets like, "rubbish," "savages," "scum," "contents of dustbins" and "creeping disease," were much in vogue.

Although the East End was an area of poverty and decayed housing long before the 1880's, the time before the arrival of the Jews soon took on the characteristics of a golden age, helped by the promptings of anti-alien agitators: "In the afternoon," remembered one resident "you would see the steps inside cleaned, and the women with their clean white aprons sat in summer times inside the doors, perhaps at needle-work, with their little children about them. Now it is a seething mass of refuse and filth . . . the stench is disgraceful . . . They are such an unpleasant, indecent people."

People became convinced, against all the evidence of government reports and independent enquiries, that immigrants were harbingers of crime and disease. An outbreak of small-pox in the early years of the new century was the signal for a vicious and largely undeserved attack on "those loathsome wretches who come grunting and itching to our shores." Jews were blamed for the prevalence of crime in the East End, although any reasonable person could see that law-breaking had been endemic in this poverty stricken desert ever since the eighteenth century. Some people blamed the Jews for the frightful Ripper Murders of the late 1880's, which terrified Londoners and did much to draw attention to the plight of the East End. It was asserted, quite without foundation, that synagogues were being constructed in major prisons, because of the prevalence of Jewish crime.

Much of the case against the immigrant at this time was conducted in the context of the so-called Social Darwinist theory. It had been popularly deduced from Darwin's theory of evolution, that not only different species, but different races, and even nations, had reached varying stages of development, and that the historical process was a sort of atavistic struggle to ensure the survival of the fittest. This led many writers to place great emphasis on "racial purity," and upon maintaining the "good qualities" of the English race – as if the island was populated with thoroughbred racehorses or greyhounds rather than a diverse people of extraordinarily complex origins. These half-baked ideas led to almost Hitlerian flights of fancy about the Jewish influx, "One sees," observed one critic, "the splendid specimens of men and women – Russians, Lithuanians, Hungarians, Slavonians – clean, sturdy, open-faced, sweet creatures; these for America and Canada – to work in the fields, to work in the factories – with their strong arms, clean hearts to be put at the entire disposal of their new country. One sees, too, the very opposite of these – filthy, rickety jetsam of humanity, bearing on their evil faces the stigma of every physical and moral degradation; men and women who have no intention of working, otherwise than in trafficking. These for England."

The working habits of the newcomers were a further source of friction. It could not be denied that the majority of them were engaged in the "sweated" trades – accepting low wages, outdated conditions, and long hours of work. Although "sweating" existed long before the arrival of the refugees, many English trade-unionists believed that the Jews were undermining their efforts by under cutting English workers and accepting working conditions which the unions were trying to declare inadequate. There was also some truth in the belief that the arrival of immigrants in an area pushed up rents and exacerbated problems of overcrowding. The complaints of shopkeepers that the Jews took advantage of Sunday opening to steal their trade was sometimes justified.

In 1905, the campaign against the immigrants culminated in the passing of an Aliens Act to control the influx of destitute immigrants. For various reasons, the Act proved to be ineffective. Shortly after the Act became law, the Conservatives were replaced by the Liberal government of 1906, many of whose members were opposed to anti-alien legislation. Little effort was made by the Liberals to enforce the Act, and the death of several of the most vehement Conservative anti-alien back-benchers weakened their cause considerably. At the same time, a series of particularly bloody outrages against the Jews in Russia made it difficult for even the most zealous crusader against immigration to deny access to the persecuted. By 1910, the peak of Jewish refugee immigration seemed to have passed, and with the falling off in numbers of new arrivals, the agitation against them ceased. None-the-less, the 1905 Act was in many ways the funeral of the nineteenth century dream of unrestricted entry for persecuted and deprived people, and the Act set an unfortunate precedent for the new century.

Of all the waves of mass immigration which came to rest on English shores over the centuries the Jewish influx which began in the 1880's seemed to be most ill-starred. Arriving in England at a time of great domestic hardship and poverty, the Jews made their way to the least favoured areas of urban decay. They brought neither capital nor skills to placate their hosts, and their arrival provided the discontented with a ready made scapegoat for their grievances. And yet there were certain factors which operated in favour of the newcomers. The savagery of the persecution from which Jews were fleeing made it very difficult for men of conscience to keep them out, and the very fact that the refugees were Jews made many critics moderate their attacks for fears of being called anti-semitic. To some extent the immigrants were helped by the fact that there already existed in the country an established Jewish community which had demonstrated its ability to raise itself to a position of considerable wealth and influence through its own efforts. Despite the initial hostility of the native Jews, their presence provided an institutional and economic safety-net for the new arrivals. What is more, a small but articulate group of Jewish M.P.'s were able to mount a counter-attack against the anti-alien lobby in Parliament.

For the British, the arrival of the Jewish aliens had been a severe test of the nineteenth century philosophy of tolerance and asylum for the foreigner. It was unfortunate that the immigrants arrived at a time when accumulated social problems, the pressures of growing foreign competition and the burden of outdated technology and institutional complacency were beginning to sour the Victorian idyll. It was too easy for the immigrants to become scapegoats for suffering for which they were only marginally responsible.

The immigrant's willingness to work, and his often ruthless competitiveness – the only weapon he had in the fight for survival – dragged him into the struggle between socialism and *laissez-faire* capitalism. For believers in the capitalist system, the Jew appeared as the very epitome of Economic Man – willing to work endlessly, accept any conditions and compete ruthlessly against his fellows in order to improve his economic status. For the socialists, the Jewish immigrant seemed to symbolize all those things which had held back the improvement of workers' conditions for so long – docility, lack of organization, and a willingness to play into employers' hands by undercutting other workers. There was only a grain of truth in these assertions, but the Jewish worker was dragged into social conflicts which existed long before his arrival as a symbol and a pawn in the struggle between two ideologies.

Jews were often blamed for the large amount of crime in the East End of London.

5 Reluctant Hosts 1905–1952

The First World War

THE ALIENS ACT OF 1905, which sought to exclude immigrants "without visible means of support" marked the end of the Victorian tradition of allowing free entry for all. The Act was more important as a symbol of the death of this tradition than as a means of keeping out aliens, for the numbers of new arrivals in the country continued to rise, reaching no less than 691,000 by 1913. It was the outbreak of the First World War that led to the utter collapse of any attempt to keep out foreigners, but the precedent for excluding people had been set, and the government was under constant pressure to introduce tougher controls.

The tremendous upheavals of the war in Europe meant that thousands of temporary alien residents were allowed to enter the country. There was also a flood of men from every corner of the Empire – Australians and New Zealanders, Canadians, Indians and Africans – who poured into the country to serve in the armed forces or to take over the jobs of Englishmen who were serving at the front. In September 1914, thousands of Belgians, fleeing from the advancing German armies, began to land along the coasts. The fact that Belgium was an ally, and the widespread sympathy among the public, made it impossible to keep these people out, and generous private charity helped them to find temporary accommodation and jobs. For a time parts of London, particularly Soho, were inundated with Flemish and French speaking exiles. Like the emigrés at the time of the Napoleonic Wars, most of these people returned home at the end of the war.

Race Riots, 1919

Some of the people who came to work or fight for Britain in her time of need, particularly those from the Dominions and Colonies, did decide to stay in the country. This is the explanation for the serious and unprecedented series of race-riots which broke out in the summer of 1919. The reasons for these outbreaks were depressingly familiar; disappointment amongst Englishmen returning home from four years of war and finding no work turned against the small black community as the most conspicuous scapegoats, and resentment was sparked off by relationships between black men and white women.

The ports of London, Cardiff, and Liverpool were the main centres of

Opposite. Wash day in an Italian area of London, 1907.

disturbance. In Liverpool, rioting lasted several days, with white mobs pursuing Negroes through the streets and beating them severely if they caught them. Similar scenes occurred in Cardiff, where white youths climbed on to the roofs of houses in the Negro quarter and threw down broken slates and bottles on the people below. Mobs of white men, many of them in uniform, raged through the streets smashing windows and setting fire to houses. These riots were very serious affairs; troops had to quell the mobs; fire-arms were used, and three people lost their lives. Damage to property was widespread. Despite the fact that all observers agreed that the black community was a victim rather than an instigator of these attacks, the number of Negroes arrested far outnumbered that of whites, and the main response of the government was to encourage the black immigrants to go home by offering them cheap berths in ships.

The Interwar Years

The tremendous upheavals of the First World War caused unprecedented movements of population. All over Europe and the Middle East, huge numbers of displaced and frightened people scurried back and forth across frontiers like ants in an overturned nest. Millions of people were on the move – Greeks, Turks and Armenians, Germans and Slavs, Jews and Arabs, Poles and Russians. All over Europe there were trains full of refugees, huge camps bursting with the human debris of four years of war, and lines of displaced people carrying their possessions in their hands. Apart from the disruption of the War, the Russian Revolution had sent nearly two million emigrés fleeing into exile, and by 1920, over 200,000 of them, for the most part young and educated men, had settled in France. Many of these Russian emigrés had outstanding gifts to offer any country that was willing to accept them. Numbered amongst them were great musicians like Rachmaninov and Stravinsky, the entire company of Diaghilev's Ballet Russe, and an army of doctors, engineers, professors, and skilled people of many kinds. It was ironical that the only country that closed its doors to refugees at this time when generosity was most required, was England, the haven of so many persecuted exiles in the nineteenth century.

The closed door was the Aliens Act of 1920. This very stringent piece of legislation had been pushed through Parliament in an upsurge of panic following the alien influx during the War. Unlike the Act of 1905 it had no loopholes: No alien could land in the country without the permission of an immigration officer, and then only at a selected port of entry; any alien who was medically unfit, or who could not support himself, was to be refused entry; strict regulations were to be enforced for the registration and control of any alien who did manage to get in. The 1920 Act was merciless in its exclusion of most types of refugee, and the numbers of immigrants entering the country fell to a few thousand a year in the period between the wars. Thousands were to suffer anxiety, hardship, and even death as a result of its pitiless enforcement.

When the Nazis came to power in 1933, they began the systematic persecution of the German Jews. Jews were dismissed from their jobs,

In 1914, thousands of Belgian refugees fled from the advancing German armies and sought refuge in England.

had their businesses confiscated, and suffered increasing violence and abuse. Few Jews could foresee the mass exterminations that were to come later, but many began to leave Germany, realizing that life under the Nazis would soon become impossible for them. In this time of desperate need, Jews wishing to escape to England found their way blocked by the 1920 Act, which excluded all but the rich and those who were lucky enough to find an English sponsor who could guarantee them a job. The Jewish community in England rallied to the support of their persecuted German and Austrian brethren, but many were condemned to stay in the Third Reich because of difficulties in getting clearance to enter Britain.

After July 1938, when Nazi persecution increased the flow of refugees the British government began to enforce the anti-alien legislation with even greater rigour, and many refugees found themselves trapped in a

Anti-semitic posters in Germany, 1930s (*below*). Thousands of
Jews fled from persecution to England (*above*). Sigmund Freud,
the psychologist (*right*), was one of many eminent Jews who came
to England.

maze of bureaucracy and red-tape while the jaws of the Nazi wolves closed relentlessly round them. Francesca Wilson, who did so much to help people escaping from Nazi persecution, describes a tragic and by no means unusual case: "In June 1939," she writes, "I posted guarantees to two Austrian Jews. One was a gifted youth I had known since he was a child, then a medical student; the other the son of an Austrian publisher. These guarantees had to be presented to the nearest British Consul who would (1) make enquiries about the applicant, and (2) write to the Home Office to ask if the guarantor were trustworthy . . . With luck the visas were granted within a couple of months, but now both the Home Office and the Consulates were flooded out with applications. In the two cases mentioned the visas had not been granted by September 1st when war broke out. Neither of the young men was ever heard of again. One of them was in the French internment camp at Gurs. When the Germans took over this camp in 1942, they shot the Jews."

Only in the case of children did the British government show some flexibility and compassion. Nearly 10,000 Jewish children were allowed in after the particularly bloody anti-Jewish brutalities of November 1938. Despite a violent Press campaign by people who disapproved of the politics of their Republican parents, 4,000 Basque children – refugees of the Spanish Civil War – were brought in during 1937. The attitude of the British people towards these refugees was very different to that of the government, and these children, many of them orphans, were received with generous hospitality.

Other favoured refugees who were able to overcome the barriers of the anti-alien legislation were the displaced university professors and scholars who escaped from Nazi persecution with the aid of the Academic Assistance Council. This body, which was set up by Sir William Beveridge in 1933, was responsible for rescuing hundreds of distinguished scholars and finding them employment in Universities and research institutions. As a result of this scheme the country was enriched by the arrival of distinguished men in almost every field of learning: eminent psychologists like Sigmund Freud; scientists, who made important contributions to nuclear and medical research; scholars, who developed new disciplines like the study of Art History – a task made easier by the transfer of the Warburg Institute from Hamburg to London in 1933.

There is no doubt that the defeat of Germany was made easier by the technical and scientific advances which many of the emigrés pioneered. The contributions of alien scholars and scientists, most of whom remained in the country after the war, were spectacular, but their overall numbers were small in comparison with the thousands of less talented, but equally vulnerable refugees who found their entry to the country blocked by the workings of the Aliens Act.

The Second World War and its Aftermath

As had been the case in 1914, any attempt to control the entry of refugees collapsed with the outbreak of war in 1939. Once again the coasts of England witnessed the arrival of thousands of people fleeing from the advancing German armies. On this occasion, almost every European nationality was represented amongst them. Huge numbers of French, Belgian, and Polish troops were evacuated with the British army from the beaches of Dunkirk. There was an influx of Jews from Holland, France, Belgium and Denmark, escaping before the Nazis could begin to round them up. Later, when Hitler invaded Norway, Greece, and Yugoslavia, yet more nationalities were added to the cosmopolitan community of exiles who languished in transit camps, barracks, and temporary homes all over the country, awaiting the day when they would return to their native lands.

By 1943, there were 114,000 civilian refugees on British soil, apart from the large number of foreign troops who were attached to the British Army. Government statistics put their numbers at this time as follows:

Austrians and Germans (mainly Jews)			..		..	..	25,000
Belgians..	..	..	..	..	..	..	15,000
Czechs ..	..	..	..	..	..	..	10,000
Danes ..	..	..	..	..	..	..	3,000
Dutch ..	..	..	..	..	..	..	7,000
French ..	..	..	..	..	..	..	12,000
Greeks ..	..	..	..	..	..	..	2,000
Luxembourgers		..	..	..	..	..	200
Norwegians	..	..	..	..	..	..	10,000
Poles ..	..	..	..	..	..	..	8,000
Yugoslavs	..	..	..	..	..	..	200
Allied Seamen ..	..	..	..	..	..	20,000
Other Europeans	..	..	..	..	..	2,000

The problems of coping with these people, in a country that was suffering shortages of everything necessary for life, were considerable. Many refugees formed a useful addition to the labour-force, serving the war effort in factories and offices, or putting their skills to use as doctors, technicians or scientists; there were many children, old people, and invalids amongst them, however, who had to be looked after, educated and given medical attention. Children were fitted into the school system, and university entrance requirements were waived to allow refugee students to carry on their studies. Thousands of English families opened their doors to take in orphans and refugee families, and the various "governments in exile" which sprang up in London did much to employ and look after their nationals.

With the coming of peace, the patterns of 1815 and 1918 were repeated, and only a few of the wartime exiles, in this case mainly Jews, remained in their country of refuge. Most of them either returned to their former homes, or moved to countries which offered greater opportunities – the United States, Canada, or Australia. It was after the war that two developments occurred that were of much greater significance to the history of immigration than the war itself. The first stemmed from problems presented by the thousands of Poles who had fought on the allied side in the war. The second concerned the future of the army of stateless and displaced people who had been stranded in the storms of the previous six years.

Polish Immigrants

Although it was a Pole, Jan Laski (John A'Lasco) who was one of the leaders of the sixteenth century Protestant refugees, there were very few Poles among the immigrants to these shores until the nineteenth century. In 1795, after successive partitions by the Russians, Prussians, and Austrians, the Polish state disintegrated. In the next two centuries, Poland was rivalled only by Ireland in the numbers of its citizens who were forced to leave by economic hardship and persecution. In England, there was great sympathy for the heroic resistance displayed by the Poles in regular revolts against foreign domination, and a group of prominant Englishmen formed an association to assist Polish exiles who wished to come to England. By 1870 however, there were only about 1,700 Poles in the country, living mainly in London's East End, Manchester, and Lanarkshire.

The twentieth century saw no slackening of Polish emigration, and by 1939, there were no less than 8,000,000 first and second generation Poles scattered throughout the world. Very few of these people came to England. The First World War brought about 2,000 exiles, many of whom stayed in the country, but between 1919 and 1931, only 758 Poles settled here compared with no less than 522,528 who went to France. The real Polish influx, which made the Poles the largest single immigrant group before the start of Commonwealth immigration in

The anti-semitism of British fascists in the 1930s led to serious fighting between Jews and fascists in the East End of London. East End inhabitants fleeing as police break down a barricade.

By 1945 there were nearly a quarter of a million Polish refugees in Britain. Poles in a hostel.

the 1950's, did not begin until after the end of the War.

When Hitler attacked Poland in 1939, the Russians, at that time allied to Germany under the Nazi–Soviet Pact, took the opportunity to annex large areas of Eastern Poland. One and a half million Poles were deported to Russia, where they were kept in terrible conditions until the Russians themselves were attacked by Germany in 1941. Stalin then agreed to the formation of a Polish army from among the deportees, and as a result 83,000 Poles of military age, and 37,000 civilians, were allowed to leave Russia. After a tortuous journey through Iran, these Poles were organized as the 2nd Polish Corps under General Anders, and for the rest of the war they fought in the Middle East and in Italy, where they played a heroic part in the battle of Monte Cassino.

As well as the army of General Anders, 31,000 Poles, who had managed to escape before the Germans closed the frontiers, had been evacuated with the British army from Dunkirk. A further 21,000 were freed from prisoner of war camps at the end of the war. By 1945, there were nearly a quarter of a million Poles on British soil, and as the political situation in Poland was still confused, most of them were hesitant to return home. The problem of their future became an important issue.

The way in which these Poles were treated made a refreshing contrast to the reception that had been given to previous immigrants. For the first time, real efforts were made to deal with the special needs of people thrown into a strange environment. In 1947, the Polish Resettlement

Corps was set up to ease the transition from army to civilian life, and a planned campaign to find them homes, employment, and education was mounted. In the very difficult circumstances following the War, a great deal was done.

By 1949, there were fifty special Polish Nursery and Primary schools, and seven Secondary and Technical schools in the country, and 4,500 Polish children were being taught in their own language. Although there were cases of skilled people being forced to take jobs far below their capacity, some effort was made to ease trade union and professional regulations to accommodate them. Thirty-three thousand dependents were brought in from East Africa, the Middle East, and European refugee camps, so that families could be reunited. Polish ex-servicemen were given the same rights as their British comrades. Although 105,000 Poles, mainly peasants, decided to return when the new Communist regime brought about land-reform, the majority of the Polish immigrant community was housed, employed and settled by 1950.

Like all previous waves of immigrants, the Poles congregated in clearly defined enclaves, situated mainly in the large cities. In 1952, there were 35,000 Poles living in London, which had been the seat of the Polish "government in exile" during the War. Polish communities grew up around Shepherds Bush, Islington, South Kensington, and in the Earls Court Road, which became known locally as "the Polish Corridor." The two other main areas of Polish settlement were Lancashire and the West Riding of Yorkshire, and there were smaller communities in Bristol, Birmingham, and South Wales.

Within these enclaves, a complex structure was created to provide as far as possible a Polish environment for the newcomers. Polish churches, shops, clubs and associations catered for their every need. "If there were two Poles alone together in the Sahara," observed Brendan Bracken, "one of them would start a newspaper," and in London over fifty Polish language newspapers reinforced his point, and served to further bind together the exile community. Great efforts were made to ensure that the new generation of English-born Poles retained their sense of separate identity, and did not forget their heritage of language and culture. The feeling among Poles that they were temporary exiles, rather than permanent settlers, was very strong.

The European Volunteer Workers

The second important group of post-war immigrants was the European Volunteer Workers. In the course of the war, millions of people had left their homes to escape from the fighting, or had been deliberately deported to serve as slave labourers in German factories. At the end of the war, many of these people found that their homes had been destroyed in the disruption of the previous six years. Far more serious was the position of people from Eastern Poland, Estonia, Latvia, and Lithuania, which had disappeared from the map altogether. These people found themselves classified as "Stateless Persons," destined to languish in wooden huts and tents in temporary camps all over Europe, while governments reluctant to accept responsibility for them wrangled over their future.

In 1947 the British government began to recruit workers for British industry from amongst the stateless refugees in the European camps. Reconstruction after the war had strained British manpower resources beyond the limit, and the government realized that by helping to solve the problem of the refugees, they could also recruit a valuable pool of cheap labour for British industry. By the end of the recruitment programme, over 91,000 European Volunteer Workers had come to Britain as a result of a huge operation which effectively combined humanitarian feelings and national self-interest.

There were many critics of the way in which the recruitment of European refugee workers was organized. Only single people were chosen to come, and in desperation, many men were forced to desert their families in order to qualify. The recruits were not allowed to choose their work, but were directed into specific areas in which shortages of labour existed. They were forced to remain in their original jobs for three years, and there were complaints that some greedy employers played upon the refugees' fear of being returned to the camps to over-work and exploit them. There were some who believed that the scheme savoured too much of self-interest, and that hardship, rather than usefulness to the economy should be the main criterion of entry. Trades unionists were suspicious that the Volunteer Workers would be used, like the poor Irish and Jews in the nineteenth century, as cheap labour to undercut the wages of British workers.

Many of the Volunteer Workers, who came to the country in the midst of the post-war period of austerity, led a miserable existence. Unlike the Poles, they were often isolated in small groups far from the security of their own people. They had been forced by cruel circumstances to accept jobs that were often way below their capacity, and were compelled by government regulations to remain in them. They were housed in makeshift hostels, in the midst of a housing shortage which seemed to make their chances of getting better accommodation remote. Many of them, like the exiles from the Baltic states, were not even buoyed up with the hope of one day returning home.

The plight of these people is brought home in the words of the licensee of a pub patronized by a group of Latvian exiles: "The Latvians are the saddest of all," he told John Brown, who was writing a book on immigrants in Bedford, ". . . Despairing drinkers. They'll drink for days on end. All heavy drinking . . . but never any violence. Those Latvians are gentlemen to the death. Some of them, I think, died in the war really. They saw too much. And now they cannot go back. They have accepted that they will die here. In that state, some people turn to religion, some turn to drink . . . Those Latvians are the most lost of all. I have one, he is deaf and dumb. He doesn't want a hearing aid, he doesn't want to know anything anymore. He just cut himself off. And now he has drunk himself out. He is waiting to die."

Not surprisingly, many of the European Volunteer Workers took the opportunity to re-emigrate as soon as they could raise the fare for the Atlantic crossing. The condition of those who remained improved rapidly when prosperity returned in the 1950's. With the benefits of the new Welfare State, their material condition was infinitely better than those immigrants who had poured in unrecorded and uncared for in the nineteenth century. The state was now fully aware of the immigrant, and had the power either to help him or to keep him out.

West Indian Immigrants

Apart from the black population of the eighteenth century, non-European immigrants play little part in the story of immigration to this country until 1952. There were small black colonies in many of the great ports, made up of servicemen who had remained in the country after the First World War, and seamen who had retired or left their ships, but numbers were very small. Poverty and over-population had made the West Indies an area of large-scale emigration in the twentieth century, but most West Indian migrants went to the United States. There were about 200,000 of them in the United States in 1924, and in the following years many more took advantage of the fact that they were

Some of the first West Indian immigrants to arrive in England in 1948.

A West Indian looks for
lodgings in Birmingham.

included in the quota for Great Britain (which was never filled) to go
to join their compatriots. There is little doubt that climate and kinship
made the United States much more attractive to West Indians than
England.

Like the West Indies, the Indian sub-continent was also a traditional
area of migration. Thousands of Indians had emigrated during the
nineteenth century, but most of them went as indentured labourers to
other parts of the British Empire, particularly to South Africa, the
West Indies, and the East African Colonies. In 1951, there were only
8,000 Indians in Britain, working as students, seamen or in professional
posts. They were outnumbered by the Latvians and Yugoslavs, and
there were nearly twice as many Ukrainians as Indians in the country.
The numbers of Chinese in the country was also negligible; government
figures put them at 1,763 in 1951.

In June 1948, the liner *Empire Windrush* arrived in Britain with 492
Jamaican immigrants aboard. The arrival of this small group set off a
storm in Parliament and the Press which lasted for several weeks. It was
extraordinary that such a panic could be caused by the arrival of 492
black men, when hundreds of thousands of European refugees had been
accepted in the previous five years, but the deep seated prejudices of
many English people were revealed. It was surprising, however, that
such strong feelings could exist in a country which had contained

virtually no black or coloured community for a century and a half.

The *Empire Windrush* incident was in fact a false alarm, and large scale West Indian immigration did not begin until 1952. In that year Congress drastically cut the quota of West Indians who were allowed into the United States, and the thousands of West Indians who had previously escaped from poverty and unemployment by leaving for the United States were forced to seek for opportunities elsewhere. With the shutting off of the American safety-valve, thousands of West Indians began to take ship for Liverpool, Southampton, and London. The era of Commonwealth immigration had begun.

CONCLUSION

ALTHOUGH THE 1950's were to witness an influx of Commonwealth immigrants whose sheer numbers would be greater than any previous movement to this country, the phenomenon of mass immigration to this country was nothing new. In terms of its impact on the English people, the Commonwealth influx was no more formidable than many previous waves of migration. Elizabethan England, for instance, with its small population, its primitive economy, its limited government resources, and its rigid social and cultural structures, found that the arrival of a comparatively small number of refugee Protestants posed formidable problems. On many occasions in the past, English people had faced the problem of coming to terms with people with alien customs and life-styles; if it was more generally realized that the Commonwealth immigrant is only the latest in a long line of migrants stretching back for over a thousand years, the latest influx might be viewed with more calmness and a greater sense of proportion.

Most of the people who came to this country as settlers in the past were refugees rather than willing immigrants attracted by the opportunity of making a better life; some of them, like the Protestants of the sixteenth century and the Jews of the nineteenth century, were forced to flee from persecution; some, like the eighteenth century black slaves, were brought here by force; others, like the Irish in the nineteenth century, were driven from their homes by intolerable economic conditions. Only occasionally, in the first part of the nineteenth century, for instance, has England been, like Australia or the New World, a land of opportunity for settlers.

The attitude of the State towards immigrants has been a mixture of greed, indifference, and hostility; rarely has it encouraged them or made provision for their assimilation. Some immigrants, like the Jews and alien craftsmen of the Middle Ages, were tolerated so long as they were of benefit to the State; when they ceased to be useful or became an embarrassment, they were exploited or expelled. The Protestant refugees of the sixteenth and seventeenth centuries were treated with indifference or only grudgingly welcomed, despite the benefits they brought to the country. In the nineteenth century the apparent tolerance displayed in the reception of political emigrés evaporated under the pressures exerted by successive waves of poor Irish and Jewish immigrants, and in the period between the Wars, when conditions on the Continent gave rise to an unprecedented rise in the number of refugees, England ceased to be a haven for the oppressed. Only after the Second World War did the State begin to adopt a policy of offering compassionate and organized assistance to immigrants; and even then there were many who believed that the way in which European Volunteer Workers were recruited savoured of the exploitation of people in desperate straits.

The attitude of the English people towards immigrants is more difficult to assess. Much depended on the economic state of the country at the time of their arrival, but on the whole, the response of the English towards the immigrant has been a depressing combination of suspicion and hostility, and anti-alien riots punctuate the story of immigration to this country with bloody regularity. Because of their geographical position, the English have been less tolerant of strangers over the centuries than most European nations, and the Englishman has always had a firm belief in the superiority of his own way of life. Complaints against immigrants, whether they were fourteenth century Flemings or nineteenth century Jews, have a remarkably similar tone, and invariably involve fears that the English way of life was being threatened.

Immigrants stood out because of their unusual appearance, dress and customs, and for reasons of security and the need to preserve their separate identity, they congregated together in clearly defined enclaves, often in the poorest areas of the large cities. Unlike the Government of the United States, the English never made any attempt to assimilate the immigrant, and a characteristic of the successive waves of immigration to this country is the way in which the government made no attempt to break down their separate life-styles. To many English people the exclusiveness of the immigrant was both a rejection and a threat to English way of life by which they set such great store.

The strange habits and customs of the newcomers outraged English people who had grown up surrounded by people of their own kind; whether it was "Dochemen" emptying soapy water into the streets, Irish keeping pigs in their back-yard, or Jews holding noisy gatherings in the streets, the effect was to increase the feeling that the familiar English way of life was being undermined. On some occasions, such as in Elizabethan England or at the time of the French Revolution, wider fears were felt that the immigrant posed a threat to the security of the state. and the Catholic Irish were always suspected of being agents of Papacy and Jacobinism. Sexual jealousies, whether directed at Lombards in the fifteenth century or Negroes in the eighteenth, were another source of friction, and many people, particularly when Social Darwinism was in vogue in the nineteenth century, feared that the "purity of the English race" was being tainted by inter-marriage with "lesser breeds."

Apart from hostility which stemmed from fear of strangers and feelings that the English way of life was under attack, the immigrant was constantly used as a scapegoat for the accumulated grievances of the age. If there was unemployment, it was easier to blame the competition of immigrant labour than to understand the complex realities of the economic situation; if there was a shortage of housing, or if rents were going up, the arrival of conspicuous foreign strangers, whether they were Flemish Protestants, Irish Catholics, or Russian Jews, seemed more significant than the larger but unnoticed influx from the English country-side; if there was a smallpox epidemic, or if crime was increasing, the arrival of strangers with different standards of hygiene and behaviour seemed to explain everything. If the immigrant was rich, like the medieval Jewish money-lender or the Huguenot banker, he was thought to be a parasite who had come here to exploit the native population; if he was poor, like the Irishman escaping from the famine, he was thought to be a parasite who had come to live at the Englishman's expense.

There is no doubt, however, that successive waves of immigrants have contributed enormously to the development of this country. Their arrival was like a series of shocks which invigorated English society and stimulated economic change.

Immigrants introduced new skills and techniques, pioneered advances in banking and business, were prominent in scientific research, brought new methods of farming and horticulture, and provided a vital pool of cheap labour at times of economic expansion. As an outsider, the immigrant was not blinded by national or local traditions, nor was he weighed down by the chains of outmoded social and economic structures. By applying new techniques and fresh ideas, or by showing a willingness to work outside the framework of existing institutions, the immigrant provided a dynamic stimulus to social change and economic growth.

Although immigrants have almost always had to face the indifference and greed of the State, the resistance of entrenched interest groups, and the suspicion and occasional hostility of their English neighbours, their arrival has usually proved to be of incalculable benefit to the country of their adoption.

SOME IMPORTANT DATES

1113	Henry I invites Flemish clothworkers to England.
1144	First Ritual Murder Accusation against Jews.
1189–90	Massacres of English Jews.
1275	Statutem de Judeismo published.
1190	Jews expelled from England.
1325	Foreign monks ordered to leave the English coast.
1337	Invitation to Flemish craftsmen to settle in England.
1381	Aliens attacked during Peasants' Revolt.
1517	Evil May-Day: anti-alien riots in London.
1555	John Lock brings first slaves to England.
1561	First settlement of Protestant refugees at Sandwich.
1567	The Duke of Alva begins to persecute Protestants in the Low Countries.
1572	St. Bartholomew's Eve massacre in France.
1595	Edict of Nantes: persecution of French Protestants stops.
1656	Jews allowed into England.
1660	Louis XIV of France starts to persecute the Huguenots.
1681	Charles II offers sanctuary to Huguenots in England.
1685	Edict of Nantes revoked.
1688	Schomberg leads Huguenot troops in William of Orange's landing in England.
1697	Huguenots establish linen industry in Northern Ireland.
1705	Dutch of Canvey Island abandon their church.
1736	Anti-Irish riots in London.
1753	Jewish Naturalization Bill passed. Strong opposition.
1765	Granville Sharp begins his campaign to emancipate English slaves.
1772	Mansfield Judgement against slavery.
1780	Gordon Riots: Attacks on Catholic Irish.
1783–8	Granville Sharp's project to send blacks in England to Sierre Leone. Fails 1788.
1789	French Revolution: Emigrés begin to land in England.
1793	Aliens Act limits numbers of emigrés to England.
1845–8	Famine in Ireland causes thousands to emigrate to England and the U.S.A.
1848	Revolutions in Europe bring wave of emigrés to England.
1858	Emancipation of Jews in England.

1881	Pogroms begin in Russia.
1888	Committee of Enquiry on Jewish immigration.
1901	Anti-alien campaign begins.
1905	Aliens Act seeks to exclude destitute immigrants.
1914	First World War: Influx from Dominions, Colonies, and occupied Belgium.
1919	Race riots in English ports.
1920	Very strict Aliens Act passed.
1933	Nazis begin persecution of German Jews. Academic Assistance Council.
1938	Government tightens controls on emigrés.
1940	Second World War: Influx of refugees.
1943	Refugees in Britain number 114,000.
1945	Poles under British command number 250,000.
1947	Polish Resettlement Corps set up.
1947	Recruitment of European Volunteer Workers begins.
1948	*Empire Windrush* brings first West Indians to Britain. Era of Commonwealth Immigration begins.

FURTHER READING

Bentwich, N., *They Found Refuge* (1950).
Cunningham, W., *Alien Immigrants to England* (1898).
Foot, P. *Immigration and Race in British Politics* (1965).
Garrard, J. A., *The English and Immigration* (1971).
Gartner, L. P., *The Jewish Immigrant in England, 1870–1914* (1960).
George, M., *London Life in the Eighteenth Century* (1951).
Hiro, D., *Black British, White British* (1971).
Jackson, J. A., *The Irish in Britain* (1963).
Norwood, F. A., *The Reformation Refugees as An Economic Force* (1942).
Roche, T. W. E., *The Key in the Lock* (1969).
Rose, E. J. B., *Colour and Citizenship* (1969).
Roth, C., *A History of the Jews in Britain* (1964).
Rude, G., *Hanoverian London* (1972).
Shepperd, F., *London 1808–1870: The Infernal Wen* (1969).
Tannahill, J. A., *European Volunteer Workers in Great Britain* (1958).
Walvin, J., *Black and White* (1973).
Wilson, F., *They Came as Strangers* (1959).
Zubrzycki, J., *Polish Immigrants in Britain* (1956).

INDEX

PICTURE CREDITS

The author and publishers thank the following for loaning pictures used to illustrate this book: Mansell Collection, jacket, frontispiece, pp. 6, 11 (top), 20, 32, 44 (top), 58, 59, 60–1, 62 (bottom), 86 (bottom), 101, 112 (bottom left); Radio Times Hulton Picture Library, pp. 10, 12, 15 (top), 24 (top), 36 (bottom), 38 (bottom), 48, 51 (bottom), 52, 65, 68, 70, 72 (bottom), 74–5, 77–8, 84, 90, 93 (bottom), 96–7, 99, 104, 108, 111, 112 (top, bottom right), 115–6, 120; Mary Evans Picture Library, pp. 11 (bottom), 63–4, 103; Bodleian Library, Oxford, p. 31; Keystone Press Agency, p. 119; British Museum, pp. 22, 25 (top), 41, 66–7, 71 (bottom); National Portrait Gallery, pp. 42, 49, 62 (top); Courtaulds Limited, pp. 46–7, 53–4; National Maritime Museum, p. 71 (top); Nottingham Public Libraries, p. 83.